THE WANNAPRENEUR

WHAT NOT TO DO IN A STARTUP

ARPIT GOEL

Made with ♥ on the Notion Press Platform
www.notionpress.com

To my daughter Seerat, for being the beacon of happiness and strength in my life.

To my wife, Lovely, whose emotional support and encouragement have been my guiding light through every twist and turn of this journey.

To my parents, for their steadfast belief in my vision and for always being my unwavering pillars of strength.

To Prof. Safal Batra, for answering my long-held questions on strategies and entrepreneurship. I only wish I had met you earlier in my career.

And most importantly, to Neha. You shaped my character with lessons of humility and resilience, teaching me the importance of being humble and to never back down, no matter the challenge. I deeply wish you were here with me today.

This book is as much yours as it is mine. Thank you for standing by me every step of the way.

Contents

Preface

A mediocre idea with superb execution is better than a superb idea with mediocre execution

It is often said that one out of every ten startups tastes success. Whether that success means becoming a unicorn, being acquired by a bigger player, or achieving a magical IPO milestone, we all know the stories of those who made it big. How Steve Jobs built Apple from a garage, how Jeff Bezos transformed Amazon into the e-commerce giant it is today, and how Flipkart became the behemoth of Indian online retail. These stories inspire us, they fill us with hope, and we often use them as benchmarks, believing that success is a destination that only a few can reach.

But this book isn't about that one startup—the 1 out of 10. No, this book is about the nine others, the startups that didn't make it. The dreams that were once alive with hope, excitement, and the possibility of changing the world but ultimately met their end. My startup was one of those. A venture that I believed in passionately, a team that gave it their all, and an idea that we were sure would resonate with the world. Yet, in the end, despite all our hard work, our dream came to a close.

Starting a business isn't a linear journey of success. It's filled with uncertainty, doubt, and challenges that we often underestimate before we dive in. The highs are high, but the lows can be crushing, especially when the dream you've been building for months or even years begins to unravel.

When I first embarked on my entrepreneurial journey, I was fueled by passion, drive, and an unwavering belief in my idea. I believed that passion and persistence would take us to the top. The adrenaline rush of building something from scratch, of shaping an idea into a product, of bringing a team together, was intoxicating. I imagined our startup becoming one of those success stories—the kind you read about in magazines and hear in podcasts. I thought that if we could just work hard enough, the market would reward us.

But as the months passed, I learned the truth: it's not enough to have passion and an idea. Building a startup requires much more—effective execution, strategy, and a relentless commitment to adapting and learning from mistakes. I quickly realized that passion and ideas alone couldn't carry us to success. The execution—the daily grind of turning an idea into reality—was where we stumbled.

This book is about the lessons I learned from that journey, the hard lessons that can only be learned through experience, failure, and introspection. It's not a story of regret but one of growth and insight. It's my attempt to share what I learned, so that others who are considering or are in the early stages of their startup journeys can learn from our mistakes and hopefully avoid the same pitfalls.

"A mediocre idea with superb execution is better than a superb idea with mediocre execution."

This statement rings truer today than ever before. When we started our startup, we were convinced that a groundbreaking idea would set us apart. We thought that if we just created something innovative, customers would flock to us. But we were wrong. A great idea alone doesn't guarantee success; without flawless execution, it can easily fall apart. Execution, when done right, is the difference between a startup that survives and one that fades away.

Execution isn't just about building a product and launching it into the market. It's about every aspect of the business: product development, team management, marketing, financial health, customer acquisition, and retention. It's about learning how to pivot when necessary, how to manage cash flow, how to build a team that believes in the mission, and how to listen to feedback from customers—even when it's hard to hear. It's a constant balance of creativity and discipline.

We learned the hard way that every step of building a business requires focus and attention to detail. In the early days, we neglected the basics—things like keeping track of our numbers, understanding our cash flow, and managing our resources wisely. We focused too much on the bigger picture and neglected the small details that eventually became the weak points in our foundation. Without the right financial discipline, without tracking metrics, without understanding how to read and react to our numbers, we were doomed to fail.

Looking back, I realize that the importance of understanding and managing numbers cannot be overstated. This is one of the key lessons I want to pass on to every aspiring entrepreneur. Your numbers aren't just figures—they are the pulse of your business. Knowing your cash flow, understanding your burn rate, and constantly evaluating whether you are on track to hit your goals can mean the difference between success and failure. It's not about having the best product; it's about having a sustainable business model that supports growth.

We didn't just mismanage the numbers; we also missed out on building a strong core team. A startup is only as strong as the people behind it. I used to believe that if you had a great idea, the team would come. But that's not true. Building a successful team requires intentionality, patience, and effort. It's not enough to just hire people who are good at their jobs. You need people who believe in the vision, who can adapt when things go wrong, and who are willing to put in the work when things get tough.

One of the biggest challenges I faced as a founder was moving away from "manager mode" and embracing the role of a leader. In the early stages, I found myself focused on the day-to-day management of operations, from hiring to overseeing projects to solving small problems. While it's important to stay hands-on in a startup, I soon realized that the bigger picture required my focus on vision, strategy, and team development. It was only when I shifted from being the "manager" to being the "leader" that our startup started to move in the right direction.

Another key lesson was understanding the value of networking. Early on, I was too focused on building the product and neglected the importance of connecting with people in the industry. Networking isn't just about selling your idea; it's about building relationships with people who can provide mentorship, guidance, and even potential partnerships. Successful entrepreneurs know that their network is one of their most valuable assets.

Finally, I learned that keeping your family in the loop is not just a nice-to-have; it's a necessity. Entrepreneurship can be all-consuming, and it's easy to get lost in the hustle of building a business. But your family plays a crucial role in your success and well-being. Having their support, understanding their concerns, and involving them in the journey can make all the difference when times get tough.

Through this book, I hope to offer valuable lessons on what not to do when building a startup. It's not about discouraging you from pursuing your dreams; it's about helping you avoid common mistakes that many entrepreneurs make. If you learn from my story, you can build a stronger, more resilient startup. As I reflect on the mistakes, I realize that failure, though painful, taught me more than success ever could. The lessons I share here are hard-earned, and I hope they help you build something that lasts.

-Arpit

CHAPTER ONE

KISS - Keep It Simple (for) Success

One of the biggest lessons I've learned from my startup journey is that keeping things simple can often lead to success. Founders, driven by passion and a desire to stand out, sometimes overcomplicate strategies—especially in marketing. While creativity is essential, there's a fine line between innovation and unnecessary complexity. Over-engineering your marketing plans can drain resources and yield little to no results.

From my own experience, I've seen how a straightforward, targeted approach can often outperform the most elaborate campaigns. Sometimes, all you need is a clear message, smartly crafted online ads, and a focus on the right audience. The key lies in speaking your customers' language in a way they understand—without adding unnecessary layers of complexity.

1.1 The "Tea Cup Marketing" Experiment: A Case Study

When we launched our product, we believed we had come up with an innovative marketing strategy that would take the market by storm. Inspired by the idea of guerrilla marketing, we thought: why not create something unique that directly reaches people during their tea breaks? Tea stalls are everywhere, especially outside corporate offices in busy areas like Noida's Sector 62 and Sector 2, and they attract hundreds of professionals daily. So, we executed what we thought was a brilliant idea.

We printed our product advertisement along with a QR code for app downloads on thousands of disposable tea cups. The logic? People would come to the tea stalls during breaks, hold the cup, see our ad, and scan the code to download the app. We believed the cups would start conversations, drive curiosity, and ultimately result in significant downloads.

To bring this idea to life, we spent lakhs of rupees printing these cups and distributing them free of cost to tea vendors across the busiest corporate zones in Noida. The execution was flawless—or so we thought.

But what happened next was an eye-opener.

Reality Check: The Ground Truth

The campaign, which looked so exciting on paper, completely flopped in practice. Less than 1% of people even noticed the ads on the cups.

Here's what we observed:

- People came to tea stalls in groups, busy in their own conversations.
- Tea breaks were more about relaxing and chatting than reading or scanning anything on a cup.
- Cups were quickly crumpled and thrown into the dustbin without so much as a glance at our ad.

What seemed like a brilliant idea in our brainstorming sessions turned into an expensive learning experience. We stood there watching tea cups—with our perfectly designed ads and QR codes—crushed and discarded without a second thought.

The Consequences of Overthinking

By the time we realized the campaign wasn't working, it was too late. We had already exhausted our marketing budget on the cups. This left us with little to no funds for social media ads, which is where our target audience actually spent their time.

What could we have done differently? A simple campaign targeting our audience on platforms like Facebook, Instagram, or LinkedIn could have been far more effective. These platforms provide tools to target specific demographics, track conversions, and optimize campaigns in real-time—all things our tea cup strategy couldn't do.

Lesson Learned: Simplicity Wins

This experience taught us an invaluable lesson: not every "innovative" idea is practical, and overcomplicating things often leads to failure. Simple, clear, and well-targeted strategies that align with customer behavior are far more effective than extravagant experiments.

So, if you're working on your startup's marketing, remember:

- Understand your target audience and meet them where they are.
- Don't overcomplicate campaigns just to stand out—stand out by being relevant.
- Focus your budget on strategies that deliver measurable results.

In hindsight, our failure was a blessing in disguise. It taught us to respect the power of simplicity and reinforced the need for data-driven, customer-centric marketing. Startups often have limited budgets, and every rupee counts. Use it wisely.

1.2 Penny Wise, Pound Foolish

Startups are often resource-constrained, and founders naturally try to stretch every rupee to the maximum. But sometimes, in the quest to save money, we end up paying a far higher price—be it in terms of time, effort, or outright failure. There's a reason the saying "Penny wise, pound foolish" exists, and unfortunately, we learned this lesson the hard way.

After our tea cup marketing debacle, we had another idea: distributing coffee mugs with our company logo. It seemed like a great plan—an effective way to get our brand noticed and encourage people to download our mobile app. Coffee mugs are reusable and sit on desks, giving our logo repeated visibility every time someone drank coffee.

We imagined people sipping coffee, casually noticing our brand, and thinking, "Hey, let me check out this app." Simple, right? What could go wrong? Well, let me tell you.

The Khurja Connection

The first step was finding a vendor who could produce over 1,000 mugs with our logo printed on them. We started getting quotes from local vendors in Delhi-NCR, particularly photo studios that specialize in custom printing for mugs, t-shirts, etc. The average cost came to ₹35–₹40 per mug, which meant the total expenditure would be around ₹40,000.

But to us, even that seemed like too much. That's when we decided to go to Khurja—a small city in Uttar Pradesh, renowned for its ceramic production. Dubbed The Ceramics City, Khurja supplies a major portion of India's ceramics and is known for being much cheaper than retail vendors in big cities.

"Why pay ₹40 per mug when we could get them at a fraction of the cost in Khurja?"

It sounded like a genius cost-saving idea at the time.

Enter Maamu: Our Vendor in Khurja

Once we arrived in Khurja, we quickly realized that most vendors there don't deal in digital printing. Instead, they specialize in hand-painted or floral designs, which weren't suitable for our needs. After several hours of searching and negotiating, we met a man called *Maamu*. Yes, that was his actual name, and he claimed to be the person we were looking for.

Maamu assured us he could print our logo on 1,000 mugs at just ₹12 per mug, using a traditional method. Instead of digital printing, he planned to make a dye of our logo, stamp it onto the mugs, and bake them in a local furnace (bhatti). The process sounded primitive, but the price was too tempting. Convinced we had struck gold, we made an advance payment and left the rest to Maamu.

The Delivery Disaster

About two weeks later, I got a call from Maamu: "Your mugs are ready, and they'll reach you tomorrow." Sure enough, the next morning, a truck arrived in front of my society with several large cartons. The excitement in our team was palpable. We had visualized these mugs becoming our brand ambassadors, sitting proudly on desks across corporate offices.

I quickly opened the first box, pulled out a mug, and inspected it. **The mug looked okay at first glance, but on closer inspection, I noticed black marks all over it.** I thought it was a one-off defect, so I opened another mug. And another. And another.

Every single mug had black marks—some worse than others.

We soon discovered the issue. The local furnace (bhatti) that Maamu had used wasn't equipped to handle such printing processes. During the baking process, ash from the furnace had stuck to the mugs, leaving **permanent black stains** all over them.

Out of the 1,000 mugs we ordered, **barely 300 were usable**, and even those had marks that were 70–80% clean at best.

The Fallout

I was devastated. We had spent hours planning, negotiating, and coordinating, only to end up with 700 completely unusable mugs and another 300 that weren't in perfect condition. After numerous heated calls with Maamu, it was clear that nothing could be done. His process simply wasn't suited for our needs, and we had failed to recognize that earlier.

What made it worse was that we had now lost both time and money. The cost of the trip to Khurja, the advance payment, the logistics—all of it added up. In hindsight, we should have gone with the original Delhi-NCR vendors, who quoted ₹35– ₹40 per mug but would have delivered quality products. Instead, in an attempt to save money, we ended up losing more.

The Lesson: The Cost of Cutting Corners

This experience taught me one of the most important lessons in business: quality matters. While cost-saving is important, cutting corners can backfire spectacularly, as it did for us.

Here's what I learned:

1. Don't compromise on quality for the sake of saving a few rupees. The long-term consequences can cost far more.
2. If something seems too good to be true, it probably is. Maamu's ₹12-per-mug promise should have raised red flags.
3. Consider the hidden costs of cheap solutions—time, effort, and the risk of failure are often far greater than the initial savings.

1.3 The Rap Video Debacle

By this point, you'd think we'd have learned our lesson about overcomplicating our marketing strategies. But startups are all about experimentation, and sometimes, that means making mistakes—*again*.

After our tea cup and coffee mug marketing disasters, our creative juices started flowing once more. This time, we had a brilliant idea: **a rap video.**

The Concept

Corporate life is a goldmine for relatable content. We'd all experienced the classic boss vs. employee drama, and we thought, "Why not turn this into a catchy rap video? It's trendy, it's funny, and it's bound to go viral!"

We envisioned people sharing the video, tagging their colleagues, and laughing about their shared struggles in the workplace. Naturally, at the end of the video, we'd include a subtle plug for our app, which we assumed would lead to downloads.

The Execution

With our plan in place, we hired:

- A freelance videographer to handle the shoot and editing.
- A local Delhi rapper to write the lyrics and perform.

The rapper was incredibly talented and delivered lyrics that were both hilarious and on-point. The song had a **catchy tune** that we were convinced would be a hit.

To save costs (because startup budgets are always tight), we decided to **act in the video ourselves**. None of us had any prior acting experience, but we figured it would add a personal touch and authenticity. Over two grueling days, we shot the video, pouring our hearts and souls into it.

When the final cut was ready, we were thrilled. It was funny, relatable, and exactly what we had envisioned.

The Outcome

We uploaded the video to YouTube with great anticipation. To give it a little boost, we ran a few YouTube ads to promote it. But since we were already low on funds (thanks to our earlier campaigns), the ads ran for only a short time.

The result? The video got less than 10,000 views before it faded into obscurity. It's still sitting there on YouTube, quietly "dancing to its own hymns," as I like to say.

The Reality Check

Looking back, this strategy was doomed from the start—not because the video was bad, but because we didn't fully understand what we were getting into.

Here's where we went wrong:

- We underestimated the competition.

A quick search on YouTube would have shown us that the "corporate boss vs. employee" theme had already been done to death. Hundreds of similar videos were floating around, many of them made by professional YouTubers with massive followings.

- We didn't understand the YouTube game.

Getting views on YouTube isn't just about uploading a good video. It's about understanding the platform—SEO, titles, thumbnails, trends, collaborations, and consistent content creation. None of us had this knowledge, and it showed.

- We ran out of steam too quickly.

Viral content rarely takes off overnight. It requires sustained promotion, engagement, and sometimes just plain luck. With our limited budget, we couldn't afford to keep pushing the video after the initial ads stopped.

The Lesson: Know Your Platform

This experience taught us an important lesson: **Marketing isn't just about creativity; it's also about strategy.**

- **Understand your audience.** We assumed corporate employees would resonate with our video and download our app, but we didn't give them a compelling reason to do so.
- **Do your research.** Before diving into YouTube, we should have studied the platform and its algorithms.

- **Don't rely on "going viral."** Virality is a byproduct of good content and strategic promotion—not something you can plan for.

1.4 The Simpler Path We Overlooked

Reflecting on our three failed marketing strategies—the tea cups, the coffee mugs, and the rap video—one thing became crystal clear: **we had overcomplicated everything.**

In our enthusiasm and drive to be innovative, we took detours that were expensive, time-consuming, and ultimately ineffective. We were so focused on being different that we overlooked the simplest, most obvious approach.

The Plan We Should Have Followed

Looking back, here's what I believe we should have done instead:

1. **Hire a Good Digital Marketer** : A skilled digital marketer could have guided us to focus our energy and resources on where they mattered most. With the right expertise, we could have avoided unnecessary distractions and targeted the right audience effectively.
2. **Create High-Quality Graphics and Videos** : Instead of spending money on tea cups, mugs, or elaborate rap videos, we could have invested in professional social media creatives—short, engaging videos, infographics, and carousel ads that highlighted the value of our product.
3. **Run Social Media Ads** : People spend most of their time online, especially on platforms like Instagram, Facebook, and LinkedIn. A well-planned social media

campaign, with proper audience targeting, would have been far more impactful than physically handing out cups or trying to go viral on YouTube.

The Missed Opportunity

The reality is that **social media is where attention lives today.** Our target audience—the corporate crowd—was far more likely to notice a sleek, well-placed ad on LinkedIn or Instagram than to read a tea cup or notice a coffee mug.

But instead of focusing on where our audience actually was, we let our creativity lead us down impractical paths.

The Lesson

What I've learned from all of this is that simplicity often wins. Startups are already hard enough. Adding layers of complexity to your marketing strategy doesn't necessarily make it better—it just makes it harder to execute.

Sometimes, the most effective approach is the simplest one:

- Know where your audience is.
- Speak to them in a way they understand.
- Deliver your message clearly and consistently.

Had we stuck to this plan, we could have saved ourselves a lot of money, time, and frustration. But then again, these mistakes also gave us some great stories to tell—and valuable lessons to carry forward.

In the end, the road to success is paved with failures. The key is to learn from them and use those lessons to make smarter decisions in the future.

1.5 An Execution Done Right (Almost!)"

One of the few marketing strategies we executed effectively was collaborating with a celebrity for endorsement. We partnered with a company specializing in connecting brands with celebrities, where, for a fee, the celebrity would create a short promotional video for your product.

We managed to secure a popular TV actress, and the reel she created was fantastic. It was authentic, engaging, and aligned perfectly with our brand. We uploaded the video on our Instagram and LinkedIn pages, excited about the potential traction it would bring.

But as luck would have it, shortly after the video went live, news broke out that the actress's brother was entangled in a major legal controversy. Promoting the video during that time felt inappropriate and risky, and we had to pull back our campaign.

Sometimes, despite careful planning and flawless execution, circumstances beyond your control can derail even the best strategies. **But isn't that the essence of entrepreneurship? Navigating unexpected hurdles, adapting, and moving forward regardless.**

In the dense forest, a tiny army of ants worked tirelessly, each carrying grains of food and building complex tunnels beneath the ground. Unlike many creatures that overcomplicate their lives with distractions, ants know the power of simplicity. The queen ant doesn't waste energy on unnecessary tasks—her role is simple: lay eggs and sustain the colony's future. The worker ants, in turn, know their duties. Some forage, others protect the nest, and some maintain the tunnels. Each task is clear, and there's no room for confusion.

One day, a newcomer arrived at the colony, a young ant that had just joined the workforce. He was eager to impress and began brainstorming ways to streamline the colony's tasks. He thought, "We should redesign the tunnels, use different materials, and perhaps even create shortcuts!" But the older worker ants stopped him. "The colony has thrived for generations by sticking to what works. Simplicity in our roles, processes, and goals is what keeps us alive," they explained.

The young ant soon realized the wisdom in their words. He stopped overthinking and focused on doing his part in the simplest, most effective way possible. Over time, the colony continued to thrive because each member performed their task with clarity and precision, without any unnecessary complexity.

Just like the ant colony, a business must avoid overcomplicating its processes. Whether it's creating products, dealing with customers, or managing employees, a simple approach—clear objectives and straightforward actions—can lead to greater success. As entrepreneurs, it's crucial to focus on the essentials and keep operations simple to achieve efficiency and long-term survival.

CHAPTER TWO

Idea is Good, but Execution is Better

A mediocre idea with superb execution is better than a superb idea with mediocre execution

In the startup world, the phrase "stealth mode" has an almost mythical allure. Founders often guard their ideas like a treasure chest, worried that sharing even a whisper might lead to someone else swooping in and executing it faster. I must admit, I too fell prey to this obsession. We were so consumed with the idea of being in stealth mode that we forgot a critical truth: **ideas are important, but execution is everything.**

When we first came up with our product idea, it felt revolutionary. We were brimming with excitement and convinced that we had stumbled upon a game-changer. But instead of focusing on executing it quickly and efficiently, we spent months perfecting the idea in secrecy. Endless discussions about features, endless diagrams, and prototypes—but very little progress in actually building and launching the product.

We convinced ourselves that staying in stealth mode would protect us from competitors. We believed that keeping our idea under wraps was the key to success. But the reality was far from it. Our competition was out there, releasing half-baked versions of what we wanted to create. Their products weren't perfect, but they were learning from the market, iterating, and improving. Meanwhile, we were still stuck in our echo chamber, tweaking an idea that had no real-world feedback.

2.1 Stealth Mode vs. Execution: A Real-World Lesson

In the early stages of our startup journey, we were utterly convinced that "stealth mode" was the secret ingredient to success. We believed that protecting our idea from prying eyes was more important than building and launching it quickly. Our fear of someone copying our concept consumed us so much that during startup events and conventions, we avoided sharing our vision. Instead, we gave vague or half-cooked explanations about our product, dodging key details in case someone might steal the idea.

One incident stands out as a turning point in my understanding of what really matters in entrepreneurship. At a startup convention, I met a fellow founder while sipping coffee. He was part of the core team of a startup similar to ours. When he asked me about our product, I followed my usual strategy—deliberately avoiding the mention of any major or attractive features.

What happened next completely changed my perspective. He started sharing his own idea. He told me he was working on building an **aggregator for marriage counseling**, where counselors would charge money per minute for their services. To my surprise, he explained his entire vision, including all the features he had thought of.

Taken aback, I asked him, *"Don't you fear that I might steal your idea?"*

He laughed and said, *"Arpit bhai, what I've learned from my startup experience is that it's all about execution. And since I've been working on this idea for months, no one can execute it better than me."*

That was a pivotal moment. I realized how misguided my obsession with stealth mode had been. **Our idea wasn't some revolutionary time machine or a secret formula that could shake the world if stolen.** It was just a product—one that required relentless execution and iteration to succeed. Instead of using stealth mode as a shield, we should have shared our vision with people who could have helped us refine it.

Much later, when I joined an executive program at IIM Kashipur, my mentor, Prof. Safal Batra, shared a valuable insight that resonated deeply with me. He said that entrepreneurs should treat every person they meet as:

1. A potential customer
2. A potential partner
3. A potential employee
4. A potential supplier

This approach can only be achieved by openly sharing the vision of your product. If you don't articulate your vision, you miss the opportunity to inspire people who might contribute to your success.

In hindsight, I realized that our fear of sharing details about our app didn't protect us—it only isolated us. We missed the chance to connect with mentors, customers, and even investors who could have offered invaluable guidance and support.

The Illusion of Stealth

In the early days of our startup journey, we were so consumed by the idea of protecting our concept under the veil of "stealth mode" that we actively avoided opportunities to pitch our idea publicly, even at startup conventions.

These events were brimming with angel investors eager to discover the next big thing. Yet, in our delusion, we believed that the only way to secure funding was through private, closed-room pitches. We convinced ourselves that sharing our idea in a public forum might lead to someone stealing it.

As days turned into weeks, and weeks into months, the reality began to sink in. Our secrecy left us isolated—without money, without investors, and still clutching tightly to our "stealth mode."

It was a hard lesson: the fear of someone stealing your idea often leads to missed opportunities. Execution, connections, and courage to share your vision with the right audience matter far more than keeping an idea hidden in the shadows.

The Lesson

Stealth mode might work in certain cases, especially for highly innovative or patentable technologies. But for most startups, execution trumps secrecy. It's not the idea that sets you apart; it's your ability to turn that idea into a reality—better and faster than anyone else.

Looking back, I wish we had spent less time guarding our idea and more time building, testing, and sharing it with the world. Ideas might spark curiosity, but execution builds businesses.

2.2 The Danger of Over-Engineering

One of the biggest lessons I learned during our startup journey was the risk of over-engineering the product. As someone with a technical background, we were naturally drawn to adding more and more features to our product. We were so consumed with making it technically perfect that we neglected the most important thing: getting it into the hands of users as quickly as possible.

The Perils of Perfectionism:

Over-engineering happens when you add unnecessary features or overly complex systems that are not essential for the initial launch. In our case, we were constantly adding features, integrating sophisticated machine learning models, and building complex back-end systems. Every time we thought we were almost done, we'd think of something new to add.

I was personally so immersed in the tech side of things that I became obsessed with creating the most feature-rich, technically advanced product. The idea of releasing an MVP (Minimum Viable Product) felt like cutting corners. We thought, "How could we possibly launch something with fewer features? It won't be good enough."

But what we didn't realize is that the pursuit of perfection actually delayed our progress. We were so focused on getting every little detail right that we ignored the most important step: launching and learning.

The "Sagrada Família" Syndrome:

We were like the Sagrada Família – a beautiful but never-ending project. As time passed, our product kept evolving and changing, and it seemed like there was always something else to tweak, another model to add, or another feature to improve. But this left us in a perpetual state of "almost ready," without ever actually being ready to launch

What We Should Have Done:

Looking back, we should have taken a simpler approach from the start. Instead of trying to create a fully-fledged product with all the bells and whistles, we should have focused on building a simple MVP that addressed the core pain points of our target users. A product that solved one problem well, instead of trying to be everything to everyone.

An MVP allows you to:

- Test the waters with real users
- Gather valuable feedback on what works and what doesn't
- Improve the product iteratively, based on real-world data and feedback
- Avoid wasting time and resources on features that no one wants or needs

Speed Over Perfection:

What we missed in our early stages was the importance of speed. It's easy to fall into the trap of thinking your product needs to be flawless before launching. But in reality, speed is often more valuable than perfection in the startup world. By launching quickly, you can start collecting feedback from real customers, make changes based on their needs, and evolve your product in the right direction.

The Continuous Cycle of Improvement:

By focusing on a simple MVP, we could have started the process of improving based on actual user feedback instead of hypothetical assumptions. Instead of waiting for everything to be "perfect," we could have started building momentum, learned from mistakes, and improved the product over time.

A Tech-Focused Mindset vs. A User-Centered Mindset:

One of the mistakes we made was assuming that adding more features would make our product more attractive. But the reality is, customers don't care about how technically sophisticated your product is; they care about whether it solves their problem. We should have focused on creating a product that was simple, functional, and easy to use, rather than focusing on adding complexity that didn't align with user needs.

Key Takeaways:

- Start Simple: The first version of your product doesn't have to be perfect. It should just solve the core problem well.
- Launch Quickly: Speed matters. The quicker you launch, the quicker you can start gathering feedback and iterating.
- Focus on User Needs: Instead of adding complex features, focus on what your target customers actually need and build from there.
- Iterate Based on Feedback: Launch with the basics, get feedback from real users, and then improve.

At the end of the day, the most successful startups are not those with the most features, but those that are able to quickly adapt and evolve based on what their customers truly want. So, next time you're tempted to add one more feature or improve the tech behind your product, ask yourself: "**Is this what my users actually need, or is it just a distraction?**"

By embracing a simpler, more efficient approach, we could have avoided months of delays, unnecessary complexity, and the frustration of over-engineering. The key to success isn't building the most complicated, feature-packed product – it's building something that your customers love and can use right now.

2.3 Idea is Good, But Execution is Better (The Real Test)

In the journey of our startup, there's one particular incident that stands out and taught me a valuable lesson about execution and decision-making.

We were hunting for an office space in Noida, Sector 62, and after searching for a while, we found an advertisement online for a rental office. We decided to check it out and met the owner, who turned out to be an IT veteran with years of experience and strong connections, both in India and the Middle East. This was the kind of person we were hoping to meet—someone who could potentially be a mentor or a partner to help us scale.

During our conversation, we casually explained our product (*at that point, we were no longer in "stealth mode" anymore*). The conversation flowed naturally, and we got a sense that he liked our idea. However, when he quoted us the rent, it was far beyond our budget, and we left politely, telling him we would get back to him after considering the options.

The Offer That Made Us Question Everything

A few days later, we received a call from him. He told us that, he really liked our idea.

But he added a twist: He didn't believe the Indian market was ready for our product. Instead, he suggested taking the idea to the **Middle East**, where he believed it would have a better reception.

He proposed a partnership where he would hold **51% equity** in the business, and we would retain **49%**. He would take charge of operations, while we would handle the technology and product development.

On the surface, the deal seemed fair. He had the connections, experience, and market understanding that we lacked. The Middle East was indeed a potentially lucrative market, and his background could have opened doors that would have taken us years to break into. However, something didn't sit right with us. Giving up control over 51% of our business seemed like a huge risk. We were still deeply connected to our vision, and at that moment, we weren't willing to take that step.

We politely refused.

Months later, when we were shutting down our operations, that offer haunted me. The thought crossed my mind—*maybe we should have taken the offer after all.* Could we have scaled more effectively in the Middle East? Would we have achieved greater success if we had taken that leap of faith with him?

I remember a story I read in chilhood.

There was a man living in a city that was hit by severe flooding. As the waters began to rise, he found himself trapped on the lower floors of a building. A car came by to rescue him, but he refused, confidently saying, "I believe in God. He will protect me." As the water level rose, he moved to a higher floor. Later, a boat came to help, but once again, he turned it down, "I believe in God. He will protect me." As the waters continued to rise, he made his way to the building's terrace. Finally, a helicopter appeared, offering a way out, but once again, the man refused, trusting that God would come to save him.

Eventually, the water reached its peak, and the man tragically drowned. When he reached the afterlife, he was upset and asked God, "I worshipped you my entire life, and yet you never came to rescue me. Why didn't you protect me when I needed you the most?"

God smiled and said, "Who do you think sent the car, the boat, and the helicopter?"

This story is a food for thought for all of us, especially in the context of entrepreneurship. Sometimes, we are so focused on our vision and the way we think things should unfold that we miss the opportunities right in front of us. We might be waiting for a grand, obvious solution, when in reality, the universe—or in our case, opportunities—are presenting themselves in smaller, subtler ways.

But that's the nature of entrepreneurship. Every decision feels like a gamble. Much like a game of roulette, you make bets hoping to recover from past losses, but you never know what will happen next. You keep pushing, even after a few misses. The uncertainty is part of the journey.

Beavers are known for their engineering skills, constructing elaborate dams that reshape entire ecosystems. A beaver's idea of building a dam is just that—an idea. It is the execution of this idea that truly makes it work. They start by choosing a strategic location where the water flow can be harnessed, gathering materials like branches, mud, and rocks, and then building the dam one piece at a time.

A young beaver once had an idea—he dreamed of building the biggest, most impressive dam ever constructed. He had a vision of a massive structure that could withstand any river current. However, as he began to gather materials, he quickly learned that size alone wasn't enough. His dam was weak in some spots, and the water began to erode it faster than he could rebuild it.

Frustrated, the young beaver sought the guidance of older, wiser beavers. They taught him that building a dam wasn't about having a grand vision—it was about careful planning, attention to detail, and ensuring that each part of the dam was solid and well-executed. The beaver learned that the quality of execution mattered far more than the size of the project.

In business, it's not enough to have a brilliant idea. Execution—planning, gathering resources, overcoming challenges, and making adjustments as needed—is what makes the idea successful. Without proper execution, even the most brilliant ideas can crumble like an unsteady dam. The beaver's story teaches entrepreneurs that while ideas are essential, the true test lies in the ability to bring them to life effectively.

CHAPTER THREE

Manager Mode

Entrepreneurs and **managers** often inhabit two very different worlds, and understanding this distinction is crucial when building a startup. Entrepreneurs are visionaries who innovate, take risks, and set the direction for the company. Managers, on the other hand, are those who execute plans, delegate tasks, and maintain order within the framework set by others.

In our journey, this distinction blurred more often than I would like to admit.

When we embarked on our startup journey, we brought with us over 25+ years of combined professional experience. We were seasoned in managing teams, maintaining task trackers, and following agile methodologies with sprints and retrospectives. These are undoubtedly good practices—essential for organized execution. But as we dove deeper into the startup world, I realized that execution in a startup requires something more.

It's not just about tracking tasks or delivering on deadlines. It's about going the extra mile—being a **leader** for your team, not just their **boss**.

The Challenge of Transition

- From Manager to Leader:

While we had the processes nailed down, I found myself still operating as a manager—ensuring the team adhered to deadlines and processes—but missing the deeper connection and inspiration that a leader provides. Startups need more than order; they need passion and direction.

- Leading by Example:

In a startup, you can't just delegate and expect results. Team members often look to the founders for guidance, energy, and motivation. I realized that leadership wasn't about telling people what to do but showing them the way—being the first to take risks, solve challenges, and celebrate small wins.

- Extra Mile is Personal:

Beyond processes and tools, the extra mile is about creating a culture of trust, empathy, and ownership. A leader's role is to nurture a sense of purpose within the team so that their work feels meaningful and connected to the larger vision.

3.1 The Turning Point

During the initial days of our startup, we were deep into product development, with tight deadlines and high expectations. As someone experience in managing teams, I knew the importance of sticking to processes and timelines. So, I set up detailed task trackers, planned sprints meticulously, and conducted daily stand-ups to ensure everything was on track.

It worked—for a while. But soon, cracks began to appear.

The energy in the team began to wane. People were showing up, but the enthusiasm I had hoped for was missing. I noticed tasks were being completed, but they lacked the spark of ownership. The innovation we had envisioned was being replaced by a mechanical adherence to processes.

Then came the breaking point.

The Crisis

We were preparing for a critical milestone—a demo for a potential investor. It was a chance to showcase our product and secure funding. Everyone knew how important it was, but as the deadline approached, tensions grew.

One evening, during a late-night coding session, I overheard a team member, sigh deeply and say to another, *"I don't even know why we're pushing so hard. What difference will it make?"*

That hit me hard. Here we were, working on something I believed had the potential to change lives, and yet my team didn't share that belief. It wasn't their fault—they were doing their jobs, but they didn't see the why.

I realized that I had been managing them but not leading them

The Change

The next morning, I called for an impromptu team meeting. But this time, there was no agenda, no task tracker, no timelines. Instead, I shared the vision behind our startup—the *real* reason we were doing this.

I told them about how the idea had come to life, the problem we were solving, and the impact it could have on people's lives. I talked about the nights I had spent imagining how our product could make someone's life easier, how it could open doors for others, and why it was worth the struggle.

Then, I did something I hadn't done before: I asked *them* why they joined us.

One by one, they shared their reasons. Some wanted to be part of something innovative, others believed in the problem we were solving, and a few wanted to grow and learn in a dynamic environment.

By the end of the meeting, the energy in the room was completely different. The same team member who had been so disillusioned, said, *"Now I get it. Let's make this happen."*

3.2 Old Habits Die Hard

Validation: The Manager's Habit That Becomes a Trap

As managers, we often operate in environments where recognition and validation fuel our sense of accomplishment. Whether it's a pat on the back during team meetings, a stellar performance review, or achieving a coveted KPI, these affirmations feel good. They're proof that we're doing things right.

But here's the challenge: when we transition into entrepreneurship, this need for validation doesn't disappear. It evolves—and in the age of social media, it becomes louder. Platforms like LinkedIn for corporate professionals, Instagram and YouTube for creators, and even Facebook for retirees have turned into stages where everyone wants to showcase their achievements.

I'll admit, I am no exception. When I updated my LinkedIn profile to say *"Co-founder,"* I was thrilled. The congratulatory comments, the messages of admiration, the sudden attention—it was intoxicating. I felt like I had made it, even though, deep down, I knew the journey had just begun.

The Social Media Illusion: Validation as a Goal

We began attending startup events, posting updates, and even exploring paid features on startup magazines. These publications charge hefty fees to showcase startups, but they promise visibility and credibility. At the time, it seemed worth it. After all, who doesn't want the world to know about their big leap into entrepreneurship?

For a while, we were swept up in the thrill. We were part of the *"startup world"* I had admired for so long, and the visibility felt like progress. But over time, we realized something unsettling: We were spending more energy showcasing the dream than building it.

The more time we spent chasing likes, comments, and magazine features, the further we drifted from the real work that needed to be done. It hit me that these platforms—and the validation they bring—are temporary. They offer moments of applause but no real substance.

When Validation Becomes a Distraction

One turning point for me came when I spoke to a mentor. We had just launched our product, and I was excited. I called him and asked if I should invest in publishing our story on a popular startup news website. His response was blunt:

"Arpit, these things look good initially, but they don't help in the long run. Focus on your product and its execution. That's where success lies."

His words were a wake-up call. All the attention, the posts, the events—it felt productive, but it wasn't moving the needle. What truly mattered was building a great product and ensuring it met the needs of our customers.

The Illusion of Big-Name Validation

Another moment of clarity came during a startup event in **Gurgaon**. We met the country head of a renowned bank. He looked at our product and said something that stayed with me:

"Chhota amount mat mangna, tumhara product achha hai bada amount mangna"

It was thrilling to hear this from someone so accomplished. For days, we rode the high of his validation. We thought, If someone of his stature believes in us, we're destined for greatness.

But as time passed, we realized that his words, while encouraging, didn't translate to tangible outcomes. They didn't guarantee investor interest, nor did they replace the hard work we had to put into refining our product, talking to customers, and building a sustainable business. That kind of validation was gratifying, but ultimately, it was our hands on execution and being able to ask for that *bada amount*.

Shifting Focus: Building for Your Dream, Not for Applause

Entrepreneurship demands a shift in mindset. As a manager, you might have been trained to seek validation—it's how you measured success. But as an entrepreneur, the metrics are different. It's not about likes or shares; it's about creating a product that people genuinely need and love.

Here's what I've learned:

- **Your product comes first.** If your product isn't solving a real problem, no amount of validation will make it successful.
- **Customer feedback > Social media applause.** The opinions of your users matter infinitely more than the

likes on your LinkedIn post.

- **Time is your most valuable resource.** Spend it wisely—building, refining, and executing—not seeking approval from the world.

The Lesson

Validation feels amazing, but it's fleeting. True satisfaction comes from rolling up your sleeves and working on your vision. The applause will follow, but only if the foundation is solid.

So, step out of the "manager mode" of seeking constant recognition. Instead, immerse yourself in the messy, fulfilling, and challenging work of building something meaningful. Because in the end, it's not the number of likes or comments that define your success—it's the impact of your product and the value it brings to the people who use it.

A compelling example from nature that illustrates the transition from "manager mode" to leadership is that of an elephant herd. In the wild, elephant herds are typically led by a matriarch, the oldest and most experienced female. The matriarch does not manage the group by issuing commands or rigidly controlling each member's actions. Instead, her leadership is grounded in experience, wisdom, and emotional intelligence, which align the herd's efforts toward survival and harmony.

The matriarch guides the group to water sources during droughts, protects younger elephants from predators, and navigates the complexities of the environment. Her decisions are respected not because they are enforced but because they inspire trust. Younger elephants learn by observing her behavior, while other adults contribute by taking on complementary roles, such as guarding calves or foraging.

This dynamic mirrors what startups need from their leaders: an ability to inspire and guide without micromanaging. The matriarch doesn't manage individual tasks but ensures that every elephant in the herd understands their purpose within the larger goal of survival and stability. Similarly, founders must transition from micromanaging tasks to fostering trust, empowering their team to take ownership, and cultivating a shared vision. A startup thrives, much like an elephant herd, when each member's actions are aligned with the group's shared objectives, driven by the confidence and wisdom of its leader.

CHAPTER FOUR

Equity

4.1 Equity Allocation in Startups: Getting It Right

One of the most critical decisions in a startup's journey is determining how equity is split among founders. At the surface, it might seem like a straightforward decision, but the complexities beneath can make or break a startup even before it begins. Misunderstandings, lack of clarity, or an imbalance in equity allocation can lead to resentment, distrust, and, ultimately, the failure of a promising idea.

The Role of Equity in Startup Success

When you start a business, the concept of equity is one of the first—and most important—things to consider. Equity is what gives co-founders a sense of ownership and commitment to the startup. It's a shared piece of the company that binds everyone together, ensuring that each individual is motivated to work toward the company's success. However, equity isn't just about ownership; it's about balancing contributions, responsibilities, and rewards. A poorly managed equity distribution can be the downfall of a company, even before it's had a chance to thrive.

Equity serves multiple roles:

1. Motivation for Founders: Equity incentivizes founders to stay committed during tough times.
2. Attracting Talent: Early employees often accept lower salaries in exchange for equity, believing in the company's vision.
3. Securing Investors: Investors look at equity distribution as an indicator of a startup's seriousness and potential for growth.

Poor equity distribution doesn't just create friction; it can also deter potential investors, who may question the fairness of the setup or the longevity of the founding team.

What Is Equity? A Detailed Look

Equity, in the simplest terms, is ownership. It's the portion of the company that a founder holds, and it can come in various forms, such as shares or stakes in the company. Equity gives the holder certain rights, including a share in the company's profits (if any), voting rights on key company decisions, and a claim to the company's assets if it's sold or liquidated.

Types of Equity in Startups

1. Common Stock: Typically held by founders and employees, offering ownership and voting rights.
2. Preferred Stock: Often issued to investors, offering specific privileges like fixed dividends or priority in liquidation.
3. Sweat Equity: Represents the value of time and effort contributed, often used in lieu of financial investment.

In a startup, equity plays a critical role in aligning the interests of the founders, employees, and investors. Early on, equity decisions have a lasting impact on how the startup will function in the future. Poor equity distribution decisions can lead to resentment, disengagement, and ultimately, the collapse of a company.

Equity Should Reflect Contribution

Equity is not just a percentage; it's a reflection of ownership, contribution, and responsibility. If one founder holds a significantly larger equity share, it should be proportional to their contribution—whether that's in terms of time, effort, or money.

For instance, if a co-founder holds 70% of the equity, they should ideally invest 70% of the startup's initial capital or offer a similarly significant contribution in another form, such as a critical skillset or full-time dedication. This ensures fairness and avoids one partner feeling burdened while the other benefits disproportionately.

Frameworks for Equity Splits

One common method for fair allocation is the Slicing Pie model. This approach dynamically adjusts equity based on measurable contributions, including time, money, intellectual property, and resources.

For example:

Founder A invests ₹5,00,000.

Founder B works full-time, contributing labor valued at ₹10,00,000 per year.

Using this model, Founder B could initially hold a larger equity share, as their contribution outweighs the financial input of Founder A.

By reassessing contributions over time, this method ensures fairness, prevents disputes, and keeps the team motivated.

4.2 Founders' Agreements Are Non-Negotiable

One of the biggest mistakes early-stage startups make is skipping a formal Founders' Agreement. A handshake or verbal understanding might seem enough when enthusiasm is high, but as time passes, ambiguities can lead to disputes.

What to Include in a Founders' Agreement:

1. Equity Split: Clear rationale behind the percentage allocation.
2. Roles and Responsibilities: Define each founder's role to avoid overlaps and conflicts.
3. Financial Contributions: Proportional investments by each founder.
4. Exit Strategies: Include buyout clauses and rules for equity transfer.
5. Dispute Resolution: Outline methods for addressing disagreements.
6. Hiring Policies: Rules for involving family members or acquaintances.

Example of a Clause:

"If a founder decides to leave within the first 12 months, all unvested equity will revert to the company."

This clause protects the remaining founders from dilution due to non-contributing members.

4.3 Shared Financial Responsibility

When capital is required to kickstart a business, the financial burden should not fall disproportionately on one founder unless explicitly agreed upon.

Consider two founders: one brings financial capital, and the other offers technical expertise. If the financial founder assumes all risk, they might feel overburdened. A better approach is to align equity with contributions:

Founder A invests ₹5,00,000.

Founder B contributes ₹5,00,000 worth of code development.

Both founders share risk equally, creating a balanced dynamic.

Transparency in Financial Transactions

In many startups, especially those led by a mix of technical and non-technical founders, financial transparency becomes a grey area. One founder may handle the finances, while the other focuses on product development or operations.

Steps to Ensure Transparency:

- Shared Access: All founders should have equal access to financial records.
- Monthly Reports: Share detailed updates on expenses, revenue, and cash flow.

Real-World Case Study: The Importance of Proper Financial Governance

Consider this scenario, which highlights the importance of transparency and proper documentation in financial governance. It's a cautionary tale that underscores how neglecting these aspects can lead to disputes, financial losses, and strained relationships.

The Story of Ajay and Vijay

Two passionate individuals, Ajay and Vijay, met online and decided to embark on an entrepreneurial journey together. They brainstormed and analyzed several ideas. Ultimately, they decided to pursue Vijay's idea, which both believed had revolutionary potential.

The Initial Agreement

After discussions about partnership and equity structure:

1. Vijay revealed that he and his another friend had been working on the idea for some time.
2. To reflect the involvement of all three parties (Ajay ,Vijay, and Vijay's friend), they decided to divide the shares equally: 33.33% each.

The Change in Equity Structure

A day before registering the company, Vijay explained that due to legal constraints, his friend could not officially own shares. Hence, his friend's share would also be vested with Vijay. This revised the equity structure to:

- Vijay: 67%
- Ajay: 33%

Ajay agreed, and the company was registered.

The Financial Contributions

Ajay and Vijay contributed to the shared capital:

- Ajay: ₹33,000
- Vijay: ₹67,000
- Ajay also raised ₹12 lakhs from friends and family as part of an initial funding round.

The Key Financial Oversight

1. Lack of Documentation:

- There was no formal documentation for the allocation of shares from the ₹12 lakhs raised.
- The financial transactions were not properly recorded or tracked.

2. Delegation of Financial Management:

- Vijay managed the company's finances entirely.
- Ajay focused on technology end, did not monitor financial transactions.

The Outcome

As the company struggled and eventually ran out of funds, the burden of returning the ₹12 lakhs raised from friends and family fell solely on Ajay. Since the shares were not formally allocated and financial records were unclear, Ajay was personally liable for the borrowed money, leading to significant financial and emotional stress.

4.4 Avoid Emotional and Family Conflicts

Startups thrive on professionalism, and personal relationships can sometimes blur the boundaries. To maintain a healthy work culture, founders should agree on policies regarding hiring family members or close acquaintances.

Best Practices:

- Create a rule prohibiting family hires unless **unanimously agreed upon.**
- Document decisions to ensure transparency.

- Avoid favoritism by adhering strictly to performance metrics

4.5 Avoiding Personal Transactions from Company Accounts

One of the critical pitfalls that founders must consciously avoid is using company accounts for personal transactions. While this may seem harmless or temporary, it can lead to significant problems in terms of compliance, transparency, and trust. This practice, even when done with the promise of future adjustments, can harm the startup's financial integrity and reputation.

Why Founders Engage in Personal Transactions

It's not uncommon for founders to face personal financial challenges, especially in the early stages of a startup when cash flow is tight. Some founders might justify using company funds for personal expenses with intentions such as:

- Adjusting the amount against future salaries.
- Considering it as a loan to be repaid.
- Treating it as part of their equity contribution.

The Risks of Personal Transactions

- Compliance Issues

Using company accounts for personal expenses can raise red flags during audits or tax assessments. Many jurisdictions have strict rules regarding the misuse of business funds, and non-compliance can lead to penalties, fines, or legal actions.

For example:

Expenses unrelated to the business might disqualify legitimate deductions, increasing the company's taxable income.

Misuse of funds could lead to charges of embezzlement or breach of fiduciary duty.

- Loss of Trust

In startups with multiple founders or stakeholders, personal transactions can erode trust between team members. If one founder misuses company funds, others may question their integrity, leading to strained relationships and, potentially, a breakdown in collaboration.

- Investor Concerns

Investors perform due diligence before providing funding, and irregularities in financial records can scare them away. Personal expenses from company accounts may signal poor governance and financial mismanagement, making the startup a less attractive investment.

- Difficulty in Financial Management

Tracking and managing finances becomes unnecessarily complicated when personal transactions are mixed with business accounts. This can:

Create inaccuracies in financial statements.

Lead to misallocation of resources.

Complicate fundraising or loan applications due to inconsistent financial records.

- Damaged Reputation

Even if resolved internally, such practices can tarnish a founder's reputation in the startup ecosystem. Word spreads quickly in entrepreneurial circles, and a reputation for financial irresponsibility can limit future opportunities.

Real-World Example: The Domino Effect of Misused Funds

Consider a scenario where a founder uses company funds to pay for a personal vacation, intending to adjust the amount against their salary. Over time, such practices might escalate, leading to financial strain. The company could miss payroll, delay vendor payments, or fail to meet tax obligations—all because funds were misappropriated.

When this is discovered during an investor review, the startup loses credibility, derailing potential funding opportunities and tarnishing its reputation in the ecosystem.

4.6 Plan for the Worst

While every founder starts with optimism, it's essential to prepare for worst-case scenarios. What happens if one founder wants to leave? What if one founder stops contributing but still holds equity?

Key Components:

1. Vesting Schedules: Prevent founders from leaving with large equity stakes by tying shares to milestones.

2. Dilution Rules: Clearly define equity changes during fundraising.
3. Exit Strategies: Outline compensation for departing founders.

Example of Vesting Schedule:

- 25% equity vests after one year.
- Remaining 75% vests monthly over three years.

4.7 Lessons for Aspiring Entrepreneurs

1. Never underestimate the importance of upfront equity discussions.
2. Formalize everything through written agreements.
3. Ensure financial contributions are proportional to ownership.
4. Promote transparency in all dealings.
5. Address personal relationships professionally.

A startup is as much about relationships as it is about innovation. Equity confusion and financial misunderstandings can sour even the best partnerships. By addressing these issues head-on and putting clear agreements in place, founders can focus on what truly matters—building a successful business.

The Golden Rule of Partnerships

When you enter into a partnership, ensure that **"dono ka pet ek jaisa bhara ho."** If one partner feels they're putting in more work while getting less in return, cracks will inevitably start forming in the relationship.

Partnerships work best when both partners feel equally fulfilled—financially, emotionally, and in terms of effort.

CHAPTER FIVE

Pivot Or Preserve

The entrepreneurial journey is as unpredictable as it is exhilarating. While persistence is often celebrated as a hallmark of success, there comes a point where stubbornly sticking to your plan might do more harm than good. On the flip side, pivoting too often or too quickly can dilute your focus and drain your resources.

Knowing when to pivot and when to persevere is one of the most critical skills an entrepreneur can master. This chapter draws from my personal experience—an intense rollercoaster ride of decisions, lessons, and revelations—to highlight the nuances of these choices.

5.1 The Panic-Fueled Pivots : A Journey Through Chaos

When we launched our app, we had a clear target audience in mind: IT professionals. The product was a job platform meticulously designed to cater to their needs. We launched on Android first, with plans to expand to iOS. Confident in our approach, we executed our marketing strategies and began pitching our product to HR departments in IT companies, hoping to gain traction and onboard users.

However, the results were underwhelming. The downloads came in, but far fewer than expected. The traction we anticipated simply wasn't there. At first, the panic was mild—a kind of amber alert. We reassured ourselves that maybe we needed to tweak our messaging or increase our marketing spend. But as time passed and the numbers didn't improve, panic escalated.

This led to our first pivot: changing our target audience. We decided to shift from IT professionals to telecallers and blue-collar workers, hoping to tap into a larger, less saturated market.

Pivot 1: From IT Professionals to Blue-Collar Workers

This pivot wasn't just about a change in marketing. Our app needed modifications—both on the front end to make it more intuitive for the new audience and on the back end to accommodate their specific needs. We poured resources into these adjustments and crafted new marketing campaigns tailored to this audience.

At first, it seemed promising. The downloads began to pick up, but something was still missing: conversions. Despite our efforts, we couldn't convert users into paying customers. It was frustrating and disheartening. *The panic, now in full-blown red-alert mode, led to another pivot.*

Pivot 2: Enter Banking and NBFCs

Our next move was a dramatic shift in direction. We decided to target banks and NBFCs, hoping to capture a corporate clientele with deeper pockets. Once again, this required significant changes to our app to align with the expectations and needs of this new audience. We also revamped our outreach strategy, shifting from marketing to individual users to pitching directly to large organizations.

This pivot came with its own set of challenges. Convincing banks and NBFCs to adopt our product was no easy task. The sales cycle was longer, the expectations were higher, and the competition was fierce. Yet, despite our efforts, the results remained elusive.

Pivot 3: Built and Floated Another App

When our efforts to gain traction in the IT, BPO, and banking sectors failed, desperation drove us to make another drastic move. We took the foundation code of our existing app and repurposed it to create a completely new product—a dating app. The idea was to connect young people in near real-time, leveraging our existing technical framework to save time and costs. At the time, it felt like a quick and creative pivot, but in reality, it was a clear sign of our panic mode going into overdrive.

Looking back, it was less of a strategic pivot and more of a survival tactic. Our energy and bandwidth were stretched thin as we scrambled to put this new app together. We uploaded it, hoping it would be our lifeline, but reality soon hit us. We were out of marketing funds, lacked a clear direction, and were essentially throwing darts in the dark.

This move encapsulated the harsh reality of *entrepreneurship*—when survival becomes the only goal, thriving seems like a distant dream. As we soon realized, merely surviving isn't enough; survival needs to be coupled with calculated and deliberate actions. The dating app flopped just as badly as our previous efforts. There was no traction, no excitement, and no relief.

If there's one lesson I took from this pivot, it's that entrepreneurship isn't just about staying afloat at all costs. It's about surviving strategically. A good idea, no matter how hastily executed, cannot thrive without proper planning, funding, and a deep understanding of the market. Simply chasing survival without a clear strategy is a recipe for burnout—and that's exactly what we were walking into.

Why We Pivoted Too Quickly

Reflecting on this journey, I now see why we pivoted so often and so quickly:

- Pressure to Show Results:

With limited resources and a tight budget, we were desperate to achieve quick wins. Employee salaries and operational expenses loomed over us, amplifying the pressure.

- Lack of Focus:

In our haste to find a solution, we spread ourselves too thin, chasing different audiences without fully committing to any.

- Reactive Decision-Making:

Each pivot was a response to immediate challenges rather than a well-thought-out strategy. We were constantly firefighting instead of proactively planning.

- Underestimating Execution Time:

Every pivot required changes to the product, marketing strategies, and sales approaches. These changes were rushed, leading to half-baked solutions that failed to deliver results.

Out of Money, but Never Out of Humor

After all these pivots, the inevitable happened—we ran out of money. Salaries, operational costs, marketing, and development had drained our resources completely. It was a crushing moment, but even in the face of adversity, we found ways to keep the mood light.

Whenever we pitched our product to potential clients or investors, we had a line that always got a few chuckles: *"Humne apna paisa burn karke yeh pata laga liya ki kaunsa market thriving hai aur kaunsa nahi. Aapko apna paisa jalane ki zarurat nahi padegi!"*

This humorous yet honest admission often resonated with our audience. It showed that we had learned from our mistakes and that those lessons were valuable insights we could pass on.

The Lessons Learned: Striking the Right Balance

1. Panic is the Enemy of Progress:

Panic clouds judgment and leads to hasty decisions. It's essential to pause, analyze, and strategize before making a significant change.

2. Validate Before Pivoting:

Before targeting a new audience or overhauling your strategy, validate your assumptions through small-scale experiments, surveys, or pilot projects.

3. Set Realistic Expectations:

Building traction takes time. Perseverance doesn't mean ignoring reality; it means giving your vision a fair chance to succeed.

4. Pivot with Purpose, Not Desperation:

A successful pivot is grounded in data and insights, not fear or frustration. Ensure every pivot aligns with your long-term vision.

5. Budget for Flexibility:

Allocate resources to sustain you through iterations without jeopardizing your financial stability. This reduces the pressure to deliver instant results

When to Pivot and When to Persevere

So, how do you decide whether to pivot or persevere? Here are some guiding questions:

1. Is Your Core Problem Worth Solving?

Does your product address a real, significant issue? If yes, perseverance might be the better path.

2. Is Your Market Aligned with Your Solution?

If your target audience isn't responding, it could be a sign to pivot. But ensure you're not ignoring their feedback before making the shift.

3. Are You Learning from Failures?

Every setback is an opportunity to learn. Use these insights to refine your approach rather than abandon it.

4. What Do the Numbers Say?

Metrics like user engagement, retention, and conversion rates provide valuable clues about whether you're on the right track.

Conclusion

After the closure of our startup, I enrolled in an executive program at IIM Kashipur, where the question of how long you should hold on to your strategy and how to validate it was brought up in class. I had been searching for an answer to this very question for a long time: ***"Was our change in direction the right decision, or should we have stuck with our original execution strategy and believed in it?"***

The answer I got from my professor at that moment finally brought me some peace. He said that, at a minimum, you should hold on to your strategy for a year without expecting any major results. After that, if the data suggests that a change is needed, then evaluate it. This was a turning point for me. It's the same philosophy that we often read in the Bhagavad Gita: *"Karm karo Parth sirf karm, jeet-haar ke chinta kiye bina kartavya par dhyan do."*

This resonated with me deeply. It's similar to joining a gym. You won't see noticeable changes after just one month, but you need to trust the process. You must believe in the exercises and stay consistent. Gradually, you'll begin to see small changes in your body—proof that you are on the right track. And just like in entrepreneurship, the key is consistency. You need to believe in your product and execution strategies, stay consistent, and after a while, evaluate the results based on data.

The mistake we made during our journey was not giving ourselves enough time to execute the plan thoroughly. We kept jumping from one idea to another without seeing the impact of our efforts in real-time, just like someone who tries a few exercises at the gym and gives up too soon because they haven't seen any changes in their body.

But just like you want a good physique, you have to go to the gym and do the correct exercises on the right machines. If you went for a few days and did non-effective things, then turned around and said, "Oh no, no change in me. Let's change the gym. This gym is not good," then you'd never see results.

Before you can be consistent, focus, and truly believe in the process, you need to have the right foundation—choosing the right product, right execution strategies, and following the right path. Only then can consistency, focus, and belief come into play.

In the animal kingdom, migratory birds demonstrate the delicate balance between perseverance and adaptability—a lesson deeply relevant to entrepreneurial decision-making. Each year, countless species undertake long journeys across continents in search of food, favorable climates, or breeding grounds. These migrations, while awe-inspiring, are fraught with challenges such as harsh weather, predators, and dwindling resources. The survival of these birds often depends on their ability to assess changing conditions and decide whether to stay the course or pivot to a safer, more viable path.

Consider a flock of Arctic Terns, renowned for their epic journeys spanning from the Arctic to the Antarctic. As they navigate this arduous route, storms or shifts in wind patterns may block their way. A portion of the flock might decide to push through the adverse conditions, hoping their endurance will lead them to calmer skies. However, experience has taught most migratory birds the importance of adaptability. They sense when the effort required to persevere outweighs the potential reward and veer off course to find alternative routes.

This strategic decision-making mirrors the entrepreneurial dilemma of whether to "pivot or preserve."

CHAPTER SIX

Know Your Niche

As entrepreneurs, we're fueled by passion and conviction. While these are essential traits, they can sometimes cloud our judgment. We become so engrossed in our vision that we fail to step back and ask, *"Does the market truly need what we're building?"*

I learned this the hard way, but it became one of the most valuable lessons of my entrepreneurial journey.

6.1. Market Need vs. Product Passion

One critical realization is that passion for a product is not enough—it must solve a genuine problem. During one of our pitches to an HR professional, we proudly explained how our app could revolutionize recruitment. After listening patiently, she responded:

"Is there really a market need for real-time recruitment? If a candidate shows up two days later instead of ten minutes, it hardly makes a difference as long as the hiring process is smooth. What's more important is ensuring that the interview panel is ready on time."

This feedback struck a chord. We had been so focused on building a "cool" solution that we forgot to ask if the problem we were solving was even significant.

Another potential client gave us a different perspective: *"Your app addresses a niche market. Few HR professionals might need candidates this quickly, but for most corporate hiring, decisions aren't made in real-time. Plus, the job market is saturated with similar solutions."*

This led me to two fundamental questions that every entrepreneur must address:

1. Does the product solve a problem that people care, deeply about?
2. Is the target audience willing and able to pay for it?

If the answer to either question is "no," it's time to go back to the drawing board.

6.2. Evaluating a Product's Viability

There are two key parameters to validate any idea:

- Capacity to Buy: Does the target market have the financial resources to pay for your product?

Example: An innovative product might excite a college student, but if they can't afford it, your market shrinks dramatically.

- Willingness to Buy: Even if the market can afford your product, do they value it enough to spend their money on it?

Both parameters must align for your idea to succeed.

6.3. How to Validate Your Idea

Traditional methods like surveys and questionnaires can be useful, but they have limitations. People often don't have time to fill out forms unless there's something in it for them. Worse, their responses may not reflect their actual behavior.

Instead, I believe in a more direct and practical approach:

1. Create a Minimum Viable Product (MVP)

An MVP is a simplified version of your product that captures its core functionality. It's not about perfection—it's about testing the waters.

2. Launch to a Small, Targeted Audience

Share your MVP with a controlled group—friends, colleagues, or potential users within your network. These individuals will give you honest, actionable feedback.

3. Incorporate a Feedback Loop

Build mechanisms for users to share their experiences, whether through surveys, in-app feedback forms, or direct conversations. Their input will help you identify what's working and what's not.

4. Iterate and Improve

Use the feedback to refine your product. This iterative process ensures that you're building something your audience truly needs.

5. Expand Gradually

Once you've validated your idea with a small group, scale up slowly, testing new markets and user segments.

6.4. Lessons from Our Mistakes

When we launched our app, we skipped the crucial step of testing it with a smaller audience. Instead, we went straight to the open market, convinced that our product was ready to take off. In hindsight, we should have:

1. Shared it with our network first.
2. Actively sought feedback to identify gaps.
3. Used that feedback to refine the product before scaling.
4. Our mistake cost us time, resources, and credibility.

6.5. Differentiation: The Key to Success

My Professor, Prof. Safal Batra once shared a profound lesson about differentiation. He used the example of two sweet shops:

"Imagine a sweet shop in your town famous for its Ras Malai, sold at ₹300/kg. You're a regular customer. One day, a new shop opens across the street, offering Ras Malai for ₹ 250/kg. You call your family to share the news, but they reply, 'Why risk it for just ₹50 less? Our regular shop's Ras Malai is tried and tested.'

Now imagine that instead of Ras Malai, the new shop offers Mysore Pak for ₹350/kg. Suddenly, you're intrigued. Even though it's more expensive, you and your family are curious to try something new."

The lesson? Competing on price is tough, especially for small businesses. Differentiation—offering something unique that the market hasn't seen before—is often the better strategy.

6.6. The Role of Feedback in Validation

Building a product without listening to your audience is like shooting in the dark. It's essential to:

1. Ask the right questions: What problem does the product solve? Is it solving it effectively?
2. Observe behavior, not just words: Often, people say one thing but act differently. Use data and analytics to track real user behavior.
3. Iterate rapidly: Don't wait to perfect your product. Release updates frequently based on user feedback.

6.7 Additional Insights

Another crucial lesson I've learned the hard way is this: **launch a product or service in a field where you have expertise or prior experience.**

This might not be a hard-and-fast rule, but it significantly increases your chances of success. When you understand the nuances of your industry, you can identify real pain points, anticipate challenges, and execute solutions more effectively.

The Power of Expertise

Take the restaurant business, for example. Some of the most successful and beloved restaurants are owned or co-owned by chefs. Why? Because they know the craft. They understand the balance of flavors, the importance of presentation, and the operational intricacies of running a kitchen.

Here's what happens when you're an expert in your field:

- You Build Credibility:

Customers trust businesses run by people who clearly know their domain. An experienced chef-owner, for instance, attracts diners who believe in the authenticity of the cuisine.

- You Anticipate Challenges:

Industry insiders are better equipped to foresee hurdles that outsiders might overlook. This preparedness saves time, money, and energy.

- You Navigate Easier:

Having domain knowledge makes decision-making faster and more accurate. You're not learning the basics on the job—you're applying your expertise.

- You have better connects:

Being from the same field, your connects are already stronger and you know the right resources and people to bring on board.

6.7. Closing Thoughts

Validating your idea is one of the most important steps in entrepreneurship. It requires humility, patience, and a willingness to listen. Start small, focus on solving real problems, and never stop improving.

Thank you, Safal sir, for simplifying these concepts and helping me understand the essence of building products that truly matter.

Imagine a beehive facing dwindling food reserves as winter approaches. The worker bees depend on scouts to locate new sources of nectar. A scout bee ventures out, buzzing across meadows and fields in search of blooming flowers. When it finally discovers a promising patch, it doesn't simply return to the hive and declare the find. Instead, it performs the celebrated "waggle dance," a communication method as sophisticated as it is ancient.

The waggle dance conveys two key pieces of information: the direction and distance of the flowers. But this performance is just the beginning. The other bees don't blindly accept the scout's enthusiasm. Instead, a few experienced workers fly out to validate the claim. They visit the flower patch, assessing its nectar quality and quantity. If they find the resources worthwhile, they return to the hive and join the dance, amplifying its importance to the hive.

This iterative process ensures that the hive doesn't waste energy pursuing subpar sources of nectar. Only when a significant number of bees confirm the resource's viability does the entire colony mobilize to harvest it.

Much like the scout bee, an entrepreneur often discovers what seems like a golden opportunity—a groundbreaking idea, a potential market, or a new product. But no matter how passionate the founder feels, success hinges on execution.

CHAPTER SEVEN

Core Team

When we embarked on our entrepreneurial journey, my co-founder and I had high hopes and a clear vision for the product we wanted to create. It was an exciting time, filled with ideas and ambition. Officially, we were labeled as "**Founder**" and "**Co-Founder**"—a common terminology in startups, although, to this day, I don't fully understand why such a distinction exists. Shouldn't every founding team member carry equal weight and responsibility? But, like many new entrepreneurs, we dived headfirst into building a company without fully grasping what it would take to create not just a product but a sustainable business.

We hired people—a few for marketing and sales, a telecaller, and a couple of app developers. These were necessary roles, critical to our operations. Yet, in hindsight, we made a glaring mistake: we didn't think of them as our core team members. To us, they were employees—people we paid to do a job, not partners who shared in our vision or believed in the product with the same intensity that we did. Maybe it was the instinct of former managers kicking in. Or perhaps it was an unconscious belief that no one could care about the product as much as we did. Whatever the reason, we failed to create a team that could truly push the boundaries with us.

7.1 The Problem With the "Employee Mindset"

When you treat your team as employees, they perceive themselves that way. And naturally, their actions reflect that perception. You'll see behaviors like unplanned leaves or an attitude of doing "only as much work as their salary justifies." I don't blame them; they were right in doing so. If I had been in their position, I might have done the same.

This was a painful realization, one that only came to me after months of frustration. As founders, we often wondered why people didn't put in the same energy as we did. But how could they? We hadn't given them a reason to. They were employees, not stakeholders. They didn't see the product as their own. And why would they? We hadn't included them in the vision, in the passion, or in the sense of ownership that drives founders to work tirelessly.

7.2 My Own Experience as a Non-Core Team Member

This realization took me back to my own experience in 2016 when I worked for a startup in Bangalore. I was one of their initial hires, and for a time, I treated the job as if it were my own startup. I worked late nights, often without counting hours, pouring my energy and creativity into the tasks. Whether it was business events, onsite client visits, or day-to-day deliverables, I was all in.

And for a while, I thought I was a core team member. I believed I was integral to the company's success, that was someone they couldn't do without. But over time, I realized that wasn't the case. I wasn't a founder; I wasn't a partner. I was an employee—important, yes, but ultimately replaceable. When that understanding sank in, it changed my perspective not only about that job but also about the corporate world as a whole.

I learned a valuable lesson: everyone in a job is replaceable. No matter how skilled or hardworking you are, if you leave, the organization will find a way to continue. The myth of dependency is just that—a myth. This experience taught me the importance of creating a true core team, especially now as a founder myself.

7.3 The Core Team We Lacked

In our startup, my co-founder and I both came from technical backgrounds. While this gave us strength in product development, we struggled in areas like marketing and sales. These were not just gaps—they were gaping holes in our strategy. And yet, we hesitated to bring in experts as core team members.

Why? Perhaps it was fear of diluting equity. Perhaps we didn't know where to find the right people. Perhaps we were simply too caught up in building the product to realize the need for a strong foundation of people. In hindsight, these were excuses, not reasons. What we truly lacked was the courage and foresight to build a diverse, passionate, and committed core team.

Had we onboarded someone with marketing expertise as part of the core team, someone who shared our vision and was willing to hustle alongside us, we could have scaled much faster. It's not just about skills; it's about shared ownership. A core team member doesn't work for a paycheck—they work for the success of the product because they see it as their own.

7.4 What I've Learned About Building a Core Team

As I reflect on these experiences, I've come to understand a few essential truths about entrepreneurship and teams:

A Strong Core Team Is Non-Negotiable

Your core team should consist of people who resonate with your vision and are willing to go the extra mile to make it a reality. These are not just employees—they are partners in the truest sense of the word.

Shared Ownership Creates Passion

When you give someone a stake in the company, they no longer think of it as just a job. They take ownership of the product, the challenges, and the successes.

Hire for Complementary Skills

Identify the areas where you and your co-founder lack expertise and bring in team members who excel in those domains. For us, a marketing expert would have been invaluable.

Don't Let Equity Hold You Back

It's easy to hesitate when it comes to diluting your equity, especially in the early stages. But the right team members will add far more value than the equity they take.

Create a Culture of Belonging

Treat your team as equals, not subordinates. Share your vision with them, involve them in key decisions, and make them feel like integral parts of the journey.

Talk to People Around You

One thing I have learned is the importance of networking and talking to people around you. Reach out to your friends, neighbors, ex-school or college mates, and even your office colleagues. Tell them about your product and your vision. You never know—one of these conversations might lead you to your next co-founder or core team member. Sometimes the best connections come from the most unexpected places. Take feedback patiently and be open to ideas. People who genuinely resonate with your passion might just come onboard to help bring your vision to life.

7.5 The Path Forward

If you're an aspiring entrepreneur or already running a startup, my advice is clear: Build your core team early and thoughtfully. Look for people who share your passion and values, who bring diverse skills to the table, and who are willing to stand by you through the highs and lows.

A strong core team isn't just a luxury—it's the foundation of every successful business. They're the ones who will help you turn your vision into reality, not because it's their job, but because it's their mission too. Invest in them, trust them, and give them the ownership they deserve. It's a decision you'll never regret.

In the wild, the wolf pack offers an extraordinary example of teamwork and leadership, perfectly illustrating the importance of a core team. Each member of the pack has a well-defined role that contributes to the group's survival and success. The alpha wolf is the leader, setting direction, making critical decisions, and maintaining order within the pack. However, leadership alone doesn't ensure success. The beta wolf serves as the second-in-command, often acting as a stabilizing force and ensuring the alpha's directives are executed effectively.

Beyond the leadership roles, every wolf in the pack has specialized duties. Hunters work in coordinated harmony to track, ambush, and bring down prey, ensuring the pack has enough food. Scouts explore the terrain, identifying threats and opportunities, such as rival predators or a new water source. Caretakers nurture the young and protect the vulnerable, ensuring the next generation of wolves can grow and thrive. Even the omega wolf, often seen as the lowest-ranking member, plays a vital role by diffusing tension and promoting social bonding within the pack.

What makes this dynamic so powerful is the trust and synergy among the members. Each wolf understands its role and relies on the others to perform theirs. For instance, hunters trust that the scouts will accurately assess the safety of a hunting ground, while the entire pack relies on the alpha to lead them to safety in times of danger. This reliance on each other's strengths allows the pack to function as a cohesive unit, tackling challenges that no individual wolf could face alone.

The wolf pack's approach is a perfect metaphor for building a strong core team in any venture. Just like the pack, a successful team thrives on diversity of skills, mutual trust, and shared goals. Every member should know their role, play to their strengths, and contribute to the collective mission. Whether in the wild or in the workplace, the lesson remains the same: no one succeeds alone. A well-structured and harmonious team is the foundation of lasting success.

CHAPTER EIGHT

Numbers

Numbers hold immense power in the entrepreneurial journey—they can make or break your pitch. Yet, as entrepreneurs, especially in the early stages, we often overlook or mishandle them. Numbers aren't just figures on a spreadsheet; they are the backbone of your startup's story, reflecting your vision, growth trajectory, and credibility. Whether it's your sales projections, go-to-market strategy, profit margins, expenses, or long-term roadmaps, how you craft, understand, and present these numbers can profoundly influence your chances of securing investment.

In this chapter, I'll share a pivotal lesson from our entrepreneurial journey and explain why it's crucial to own, justify, and perfect your numbers.

8.1 Numbers Aren't Just Math—They're Strategy

At first glance, numbers might seem like simple arithmetic, but for an entrepreneur, they are much more. Each figure you present represents a calculated decision, a projection of your business's future, and, most importantly, a measure of your credibility as a founder. When investors review your numbers, they aren't just examining your potential for returns; they're assessing your thought process, your understanding of the market, and your ability to execute.

Let's break this down into three key aspects:

Sales Projections: These aren't just estimates of future revenue; they reflect your understanding of market demand, customer acquisition strategies, and growth potential. Realistic projections demonstrate your awareness of the competitive landscape.

Gross and Net Margins: Investors want to know how efficiently you can convert sales into profit. High margins suggest scalability and sustainability, while low margins can signal inefficiencies or high dependence on external factors.

Expense Projections and Roadmaps: This is where you demonstrate financial prudence. Investors expect you to have a clear understanding of your cost structure—what you're spending now, what you'll need in the future, and how you'll optimize these costs as you grow.

8.2 Our Journey: A Hard Lesson in Numbers

During the early days of our startup, we decided to outsource the creation of our pitch deck and financial projections to a third-party company. These firms specialize in preparing investor materials and often promise to connect you with potential investors. They charge a premium—typically ₹30,000–₹35,000—but the appeal of having a polished deck and projection sheet was hard to resist.

The process seemed straightforward: we provided them with basic data, and they delivered a comprehensive financial sheet filled with projections. However, many of these numbers were derived from Excel formulas rather than grounded in deep market analysis or operational insights.

When the time came to pitch to an angel investor in Noida, we walked in with confidence. Our projections covered every possible detail—expenses, sales growth, regional performance, and profits. Yet, during the discussion, the investor reviewed our sheet, smiled, and said, ***"Arrey yaar, is number ke hisaab se to mujhe agle 5 saal exit nahi milega. Numbers par dhyan nahi diya tum logo ne"*** His remark hit like a brick.

We had failed to validate and internalize the numbers on the sheet. They looked good on paper but didn't hold up under scrutiny. Worse, we couldn't justify many of the assumptions behind those projections. The investor's trust eroded, not because the projections were bad but because we lacked the confidence and clarity to defend them.

8.3 Why Owning Your Numbers Matters

This experience taught us an invaluable lesson: outsourcing can only take you so far. No matter how well-crafted your financial projections are, they're meaningless if you, as the entrepreneur, cannot confidently explain and justify them.

Here are some reasons why owning your numbers is essential:

1. **Investor Trust:** Investors aren't just investing in your product; they're investing in you. If you can't justify your numbers, it signals a lack of preparedness and understanding.
2. **Decision-Making:** Numbers aren't just for investors—they guide your internal decision-making.

Whether it's setting milestones, managing cash flow, or scaling operations, a deep understanding of your financials is critical.

3. **Adaptability:** Markets change, and so do assumptions. If you've crafted your numbers, you're better equipped to adapt them to new realities, whether it's a change in costs, customer preferences, or competitive dynamics.
4. **Credibility:** Overstated or unrealistic projections can damage your credibility. It's better to present conservative, achievable numbers than lofty figures that crumble under scrutiny.

How to Craft and Own Your Numbers

1. **Start Simple:** Begin with key metrics that matter most—revenue, expenses, margins, and growth projections. Don't overload your projections with too many variables; focus on what you can justify.
2. **Validate Assumptions:** Every number should be grounded in logic and data. For example, if you're projecting a 50% increase in sales, explain how you'll achieve it. Is it through increased marketing spend? New partnerships? Market expansion?
3. **Seek Feedback:** Before presenting your projections to investors, run them by close connects who are willing and ready to help like: mentors, financial advisors, or experienced entrepreneurs. They can help identify blind spots and improve your narrative.
4. **Iterate and Test:** Numbers are not static. Continuously update and refine your projections based on new data, insights, and feedback.
5. **Learn the Tools:** While outsourcing is tempting, learning tools like Excel, Google Sheets, and financial

modeling basics can empower you to take control of your projections.

The Outsourcing Debate

Outsourcing can be a double-edged sword. While it can save time and ensure professionalism, it often leaves you disconnected from the details. Many third-party firms specialize in crafting visually appealing decks and sheets but rely heavily on your inputs. This means you're still responsible for the underlying data.

Here's how to make the most of outsourcing:

- Use it for formatting and design, not for generating data or assumptions.
- Collaborate closely with the firm to ensure the numbers align with your understanding of the business.
- Treat the outputs as drafts—review, refine, and internalize them before presenting.

Key Takeaways

Numbers Are a Reflection of You: Your financial projections are as much about your startup's potential as they are about your credibility as an entrepreneur.

Less Is More: Present fewer numbers, but ensure they're robust, grounded, and defensible.

Confidence Is Key: Know your numbers inside out. Be prepared to explain every assumption and justify every figure.

Learn and Adapt: Numbers evolve as your business grows. Stay involved and continuously refine your projections.

Conclusion

Numbers are not just a means to an end—they are the foundation of your entrepreneurial story. They represent your vision, strategy, and ability to deliver on promises. Craft them wisely, own them fully, and present them with confidence.

Above all, remember this: investors may challenge your projections, but what they're truly testing is your conviction, understanding, and preparedness. And when you can confidently stand by your numbers, you're not just pitching a startup—you're building trust.

CHAPTER NINE

Networking

Networking is the cornerstone of entrepreneurial success. It isn't just about making connections; it's about cultivating relationships that support, challenge, and propel your vision forward. In the dynamic world of startups, where uncertainty looms large, a strong network can make the difference between thriving and merely surviving. Imagine a startup exhibition bustling with energy—founders pitching their ideas, investors seeking the next big thing, and industry veterans offering guidance. This vibrant ecosystem thrives on networking. But is networking as important as it's made out to be? Based on my journey, the answer is a resounding yes. From product validation to securing investment, networking serves as a multi-purpose tool that opens doors to opportunities. However, it's not just about the what but also the how of networking that determines success.

Networking isn't limited to startup events or corporate gatherings; it's a fundamental human activity woven into the fabric of our lives. Whether it's a small business owner negotiating with suppliers, friends recommending a restaurant, or colleagues sharing job leads, these interactions shape our personal and professional journeys.

Top educational institutions like IITs and IIMs exemplify the power of networking. Their alumni networks are not just social groups—they are powerful engines of career growth. Graduates frequently help one another find jobs, secure clients, or locate investors. This camaraderie illustrates the strength of networks built on shared experiences and mutual respect.

My own journey into networking came with lessons learned the hard way. As an introverted individual, I often marveled at a childhood friend who could connect with people effortlessly. During a road trip from Chandigarh to Delhi, he transformed a five-hour journey into an eight-hour adventure by stopping at nearly every town to meet a friend or acquaintance. I used to joke with him, "*The day you start a business, you won't have to worry about clients or investors. Your friendships are your network.*" But now, I see the wisdom in his approach. For years, I believed hard work alone would pave my entrepreneurial path. It wasn't until I started engaging with a broader community that I truly appreciated the impact of networking.

Networking and Startup Success

When we launched our startup, we lacked the network to give us a running start. Imagine how different things could have been if we had a network of peers, mentors, and professionals to help us validate our product, connect us with clients, or even recommend us to investors. For us, every meeting with a bank or a corporate hiring head required countless cold emails, follow-ups, and rejections. After weeks of effort, we finally secured a meeting with a bank's hiring manager. But that one meeting could have happened much sooner—and perhaps more frequently—if we had strong connections.

Networking isn't just about seeking help when you need it. It's about fostering relationships over time, offering help to others, and creating goodwill. You can't expect someone to step up for you if you've never extended a hand to them. I learned this the hard way: to benefit from networking, you must invest in it continuously. This experience taught me that the best time to build a network is before you need it. Strong connections can accelerate growth, validate ideas, and provide invaluable mentorship.

Communication: The Bedrock of Networking

While networking is essential, it's incomplete without effective communication. The ability to articulate your ideas, pitch your products, or share your vision compellingly is what transforms connections into opportunities. In one of my IIM classes, a professor put it succinctly: *"Analytics is the second most important skill you need. The first is sales. If you can sell, you've already won half the battle."*

This doesn't just apply to entrepreneurs. Effective communication skills are invaluable across professions. Whether you're negotiating with a client, presenting to stakeholders, or collaborating with a team, clear and confident communication is key. Think about small business owners—a shopkeeper, hotelier, or builder. Their confidence in speaking, even in personal settings, reflects the communication skills they've honed in the marketplace. They're always pitching, negotiating, and planning. It's no coincidence that they thrive in business.

Practical Tips for Building a Network

1. Be Proactive :Waiting for opportunities to come your way is a losing strategy. Instead, reach out to friends, colleagues, and even strangers in your industry.

2. Give Before You Take :Networking is a two-way street. Offer help, share resources, and provide value to your connections. When you build goodwill, you create a network that's ready to support you.

3. Leverage Technology : Platforms like LinkedIn, Meetup, and Slack are invaluable tools for connecting with professionals, joining communities, and sharing insights.

4. Attend Events and Meetups : Make it a point to attend industry events, exhibitions, and conferences. These are excellent venues for meeting like-minded individuals.

5. Stay in Touch : Relationships fade without effort. A simple message, an occasional catch-up call, or even sharing an article of interest can keep connections alive.

6. Be Genuine : Authenticity is the foundation of meaningful relationships. Networking isn't about collecting business cards; it's about building trust and mutual respect.

A Wake-Up Call for Techies

If you're a techie contemplating entrepreneurship, here's my advice: move out of the virtual world and into the real one. We techies spend most of our time in front of screens, interacting with people through Slack, Zoom, or Teams. While these tools are invaluable, they can't replace the human touch. Before writing a single line of code for your API, focus on building your network and honing your communication skills. Attend events, join meetups, and practice presenting your ideas. Remember, a startup isn't just about technology; it's about people. You need people to buy your product, fund your vision, and spread the word. And for that, you need to connect with them on a personal level.

Conclusion

Strong networks have a multiplier effect. One meaningful connection can lead to several others, amplifying your reach and influence. Networking isn't just a tool—it's a mindset and a way of life. By building meaningful relationships, improving communication skills, and leveraging both physical and digital platforms, entrepreneurs can create a community of supporters and collaborators.

In the natural world, dolphins are one of the most striking examples of the power of networking. Their social behavior exemplifies the importance of collaboration, communication, and alliances—principles that are equally vital in the entrepreneurial world. Dolphins live in complex social structures called pods, which are not just families but networks of individuals who support one another for mutual benefit. Within these pods, dolphins engage in activities that require a high degree of coordination, such as hunting, defense, and social bonding. One of the most fascinating examples of dolphin networking is their strategy for cooperative hunting. Dolphins in a pod often collaborate to encircle a school of fish, driving them into a compact "bait ball." Each dolphin takes turns feeding, ensuring that all members benefit. This level of cooperation reflects a deep understanding of shared success, where the efforts of the group outweigh individual gain—a lesson startups can learn when working toward collective goals, whether it's launching a product or acquiring customers. Another remarkable example is the alliances formed among male dolphins, especially in bottlenose species. These alliances are not random but are built on trust and shared experiences. Male dolphins team up to protect their territory, compete for mates, or fend off predators. These relationships can last for years, showcasing the value of long-term partnerships. For entrepreneurs, this mirrors the importance of building strategic alliances with co-founders, investors, or collaborators who align with your vision. Dolphins also use a sophisticated system of communication, which includes unique "signature whistles" that act like names. This allows them to recognize and maintain connections with specific individuals over long distances. Such personalized communication is a reminder for startups to prioritize clear, targeted messaging when networking. Whether you're pitching to investors or connecting with customers, tailoring your communication can strengthen relationships and open doors. Social learning among dolphins further demonstrates the power of networks. For instance, some dolphins use sponges as tools to protect their snouts while foraging on the seafloor—a behavior passed down through social bonds. This is akin to the knowledge-sharing aspect of human networking, where experienced entrepreneurs mentor newcomers, passing on lessons that save time and resources. In the entrepreneurial world, just as in a dolphin pod, the strength of your network can significantly impact your success. Strong connections can open doors to clients, investors, and collaborators while providing support during challenges. Dolphins teach us that networking isn't just about forming connections; it's about nurturing them, communicating effectively, and working collaboratively toward shared goals. By embracing these principles, startups can not only survive but thrive in the competitive business ecosystem.

CHAPTER TEN

Cashflow

Cashflow is often called the lifeblood of any business. While profits indicate the overall success of a company, cashflow reflects its immediate health. A profitable business can still fail if it doesn't have enough cash to pay its bills. Understanding, managing, and optimizing cashflow is crucial for entrepreneurial success.

10.1 Revenue, Profit, and Cashflow: What's the Difference?

Revenue: Revenue is the top line of a business's income statement, reflecting the total sales made over a period. It doesn't account for the costs or expenses incurred in generating those sales. For instance, if a startup generates ₹1,000,000 in sales but spends ₹700,000 on production, revenue is ₹1,000,000, but profit is lower, after subtracting the costs.

Profit: Profit is the financial gain after subtracting all expenses—such as operational costs, taxes, and interest—from revenue. There are typically two types of profit:

- Gross Profit: The amount left after subtracting the cost of goods sold (COGS) from revenue. It gives insight into the efficiency of a company's core business operations.
- Net Profit: The bottom line, which reflects the total earnings after all expenses are deducted, including operational costs, taxes, and interest.

Cashflow: While revenue and profit are essential, cashflow is the real-time measure of liquidity. Cashflow refers to the movement of cash into and out of your business. It tracks the actual cash available to fund operations, invest in growth, pay debts, and survive downturns. Cashflow is crucial because a business may be profitable on paper but fail if it doesn't have enough liquid assets to meet its day-to-day needs.

Revenue tells you how much you're selling. Profit shows you how much you're earning after expenses. Cashflow, however, ensures you have enough money to keep the business running day-to-day.

10.2 The Evolving Focus in India's Startup Scenario

India's startup ecosystem has evolved rapidly over the past decade. Initially, the focus was solely on revenue growth—getting as many customers as possible and scaling the business. In the early 2010s, many investors and entrepreneurs believed that revenue generation was the ultimate indicator of startup success. Startups were valued based on their growth trajectory, often disregarding profitability. **The mantra was: "Grow fast, and worry about profits later."**

This revenue-first approach was particularly common in sectors like e-commerce, food delivery, and fintech, where scalability and market share were the primary goals. This model worked well during times when funding was abundant, and investors were more concerned with market capture than immediate returns.

However, over time, the dynamics of the startup ecosystem began to shift. As funding became more competitive and the market matured, investors began to demand more sustainable business models. In recent years, the focus has moved away from sheer revenue growth to profitability. The rise of unit economics and sustainable growth models signaled this shift. Founders started paying more attention to controlling costs, optimizing operations, and driving profit margins. The growth-at-all-costs mentality began to lose its appeal as investors grew wary of perpetual losses.

The New Era: Cashflow Over Profit

Fast forward to today, and the most important metric for a startup is now cashflow. In an uncertain funding environment, where venture capitalists are becoming more cautious, cashflow has emerged as the critical factor in startup success.

Startups now face greater pressure to prove that they can generate cash without relying solely on external capital. Positive cashflow is what enables businesses to grow sustainably without constantly seeking funding. More and more, investors and founders alike are focusing on cashflow management—understanding when and how cash enters and exits the business.

The primary reason for this shift is the uncertainty in external funding. Investors are no longer as willing to back companies that are growing quickly but are struggling to convert revenue into cash. Furthermore, many early-stage startups are finding it difficult to secure funding at the levels they once did. The influx of funding during the boom years has slowed, and venture capital firms are now more selective about where they place their money.

The shift to cashflow focus also comes from the realization that profitability is not enough. A startup may be profitable but still face a cash crunch due to poor management of cashflow. In fact, many startups that were once highly profitable on paper have failed because they did not have enough cash to cover short-term operational expenses or reinvest in the business. Cashflow is what keeps the wheels turning on a day-to-day basis.

Additionally, the cashflow-centric model aligns better with financial independence. Startups that manage to generate consistent positive cashflow can reinvest those earnings into their operations, growth, or innovation, without the need for external investors. This allows founders to retain more control over their businesses and makes them less reliant on outside capital.

10.3 Our Startup Journey: A Lesson in Cashflow Management

When we started our journey, we had an initial fund of around ₹20 lakhs, raised from a combination of friends, family, and our own investments. At the outset, it felt like we had enough capital to fuel our startup and drive the business toward success. We had big ambitions, and with these funds, we aimed to achieve significant market visibility. However, we soon realized that our focus was misplaced, and the importance of cashflow wasn't at the forefront of our minds.

The Marketing Spending Trap

In the beginning, we allocated a substantial portion of our funds to marketing strategies, hoping to generate brand awareness and customer traction quickly. As discussed in the first chapter, we invested heavily in marketing campaigns. While marketing is essential, we failed to balance it with the need for sustainable revenue generation. In hindsight, cashflow management should have been our first priority—not just in terms of how to spend but also in ensuring that every rupee spent was contributing to building a more robust revenue stream.

What went wrong here? We were pouring money into marketing campaigns, but without a clear customer acquisition model or a direct path to revenue. As a result, we weren't generating sufficient cashflow to sustain the business in the long run. Our spending was largely focused on making a market presence for ourselves than our actual growth, which gradually ate into our working capital.

High Overheads and Employee Salaries

As our team grew, so did our operational expenses. We were paying over ₹1 lakh in salaries to employees, but we didn't have a clear path to revenue that would cover these costs. Without understanding the core concept of cashflow, we failed to align our expenses with the actual cash coming in. This situation is unfortunately common in startups, where there is a rush to scale quickly but without the financial backing to do so sustainably.

We focused more on growth and less on how to maintain liquidity. We assumed that things would turn around eventually, but without managing our cashflow, we were trapped in a cycle of continuous spending. Our expenses exceeded the revenue, and as we had no buffer of working capital or contingency plan, the inevitable happened.

The Consequences: Letting Go of Employees and the Office

The first hard decision we had to make was letting go of employees. We were forced to cut down on the team size, as we could no longer afford the salary expenses. This was one of the most difficult phases of our startup journey. We realized that without steady revenue and proper cashflow management, we were unable to sustain even the basic operations of the business.

The next step was to let go of our office space. With fewer employees and limited revenue, we couldn't justify the overhead costs of maintaining a physical office. Again, this decision reflected how badly we had missed the mark on cashflow management. We learned the hard way that in the early stages of a startup, controlling fixed costs—like salaries and office expenses—was critical for survival.

10.4 The Key Takeaway: Focus on Revenue and Cashflow First

Looking back, the most critical mistake we made was focusing too much on fame game and marketing and not enough on revenue generation. Cashflow is the most crucial factor for a startup's survival, and without it, no business can sustain itself in the long run. It became clear that our first priority should have been establishing a steady stream of revenue—no matter how small—that could support our daily expenses and operations.

Additionally, we should have paid more attention to cashflow forecasting, where we could predict cash inflows and outflows more effectively. This would have helped us better manage our funds and avoid the liquidity crisis we faced. Revenue generation, profitability, and cashflow need to go hand in hand, with a clear understanding of how to convert marketing spend into actual earnings.

Our journey taught us the hard truth about the importance of cashflow. While we were focused on growing the business, we should have been more mindful of ensuring that every step, every expense, and every initiative contributed to a positive cashflow. We learned that no matter how strong the idea or the vision, it all boils down to financial discipline, especially in a startup environment where resources are limited.

Squirrels demonstrate an excellent approach to managing revenue and cashflow in the natural world. During the warmer months, they gather and store food, which acts as their "revenue." They prepare for times when resources are scarce, such as the winter months when fresh food is not readily available. This strategy is a direct parallel to managing cashflow in business. Just like how a business must generate income when opportunities are abundant, squirrels take in resources during peak times and "save" them for the leaner months.

This foresight allows squirrels to ensure their survival, just as businesses need to balance their inflow (revenue) with their outflow (expenses). The key is the timing—squirrels don't spend all their gathered food immediately; they ration it for the future. Similarly, businesses need to plan their cashflow in a way that sustains them when revenue dips, ensuring that they have reserves for when incoming cash is low.

Without this balance and foresight, squirrels risk running out of food when it is needed most. Similarly, businesses that fail to manage their cashflow carefully can face critical shortages that hinder their ability to operate. In both cases, it's the ability to manage inflow and outflow over time that ensures long-term survival and success.

CHAPTER ELEVEN

Mentor

In India, the concept of mentorship is deeply ingrained in our culture, dating back thousands of years. We have always revered figures who guide, teach, and nurture others to succeed. These figures, often referred to as "Guru," have played pivotal roles in shaping the paths of countless individuals throughout history. Whether it was Guru Dronacharya who mentored Arjun or Chanakya who guided Chandragupta Maurya, the idea of a mentor has been an essential part of our society for centuries. These mentors were not just teachers but also companions who offered wisdom, practical advice, and life lessons. I have always strongly believed in the power of mentorship, especially in the world of entrepreneurship.

As an entrepreneur, the path is seldom clear, and navigating the complexities of building and scaling a startup can be daunting. However, the value of having a mentor cannot be overstated. Let's delve deeper into the concept of mentorship in the realm of entrepreneurship, how it shapes your journey, and why it is so crucial.

The Role of a Mentor in Entrepreneurship

At the very core, mentorship in entrepreneurship is about guidance, expertise, and support. The role of a mentor is to offer practical advice, help make crucial decisions, and provide clarity when things get overwhelming. They do not just tell you what to do; they share their experiences and teach you how to make better choices based on their own successes and failures.

Now, let's take a step back and think about whether you truly need a mentor. If you are someone who feels confident that you can walk the entrepreneurial path entirely on your own, with all the tools, skills, and knowledge, then congratulations—you are one of the rare few. But remember, it is said *"If you're the smartest person in the room, you're in the wrong room."*

However, if you are like me—someone who believes in learning from the experiences of others, who understands that the journey of entrepreneurship is fraught with pitfalls, and who seeks wisdom from those who have been through it all—then this chapter is for you. For many entrepreneurs, having a mentor is not just beneficial but often essential.

The Importance of Mentorship in My Startup Journey

Reflecting on my own startup journey, I realize that one of the biggest challenges we faced was the lack of a mentor. While we had strong technical expertise and the drive to succeed, we lacked the necessary guidance to navigate the other equally important aspects of entrepreneurship—marketing, sales, and strategic business decisions. We were brilliant in technology but struggled to translate that into business growth. Looking back, I now understand how valuable it would have been to have a mentor by our side from the beginning, someone who could have guided us on where to focus our efforts and resources.

In the initial stages, our primary focus was on developing the product. We believed that once we had a great product, customers would naturally come. However, we were so focused on the technical side that we didn't pay enough attention to the bigger picture. We were spending significant amounts on marketing strategies, which I mentioned in the first chapter, without fully understanding the impact of our investments. In retrospect, having a mentor, particularly someone experienced in sales and marketing, would have been invaluable. They could have helped us understand how to target the right audience, allocate our resources more efficiently, and craft strategies that would actually deliver results. Instead, we burned through our funds on marketing activities that didn't yield the desired outcomes, all while neglecting the critical aspect of cashflow management.

The biggest mistake we made was not having someone to challenge our assumptions, someone who could have pointed out that generating revenue should have been our primary focus before anything else. We were so caught up in building and testing our product that we never paused to assess how we would generate income and sustain our operations. A mentor, with their experience and foresight, could have helped us avoid many of these mistakes. They would have guided us in terms of setting realistic expectations, understanding the market dynamics, and pacing our growth in a way that aligned with our financial realities.

A Valuable Lesson: The Importance of Spending on the Right Things

I remember an event where I met a young entrepreneur who had recently left his job in London to return to India and build a platform connecting startups with industry mentors. Initially, I was perplexed. *Why would any startup, already strapped for cash, spend money on mentorship services?* I couldn't understand it at the time. But over time, I began to appreciate the long-term value of such an investment.

This entrepreneur's platform was designed to offer startups the opportunity to connect with mentors who could provide strategic guidance and help navigate the challenges of building a business. At first, I viewed this as an unnecessary expenditure, especially when cash was tight. However, as I interacted with him and learned more about his journey, I realized that he was investing in something crucial. He understood that having the right mentor could save years of trial and error. Mentorship isn't just about advice—it's about accelerating your growth by learning from others who have already faced the challenges you're likely to encounter.

I also realized that mentorship can prevent costly mistakes. When you don't have a mentor, you're left to figure things out on your own, and that's where the risk lies. You may spend money, time, and effort on the wrong things, as we did in our startup. But with the guidance of a mentor, you are less likely to make these costly mistakes. They help you focus on what matters, prioritize your efforts, and allocate resources wisely.

The Right Mentor Can Help You Avoid Pitfalls

The right mentor doesn't just offer advice—they offer perspective. They help you see things from a different angle, challenge your assumptions, and force you to think critically about your business. They push you to refine your strategies, set clearer goals, and hold you accountable.

For example, during our startup journey, a mentor could have helped us make better financial decisions. Rather than spending money on untested marketing strategies or hiring employees without a clear plan for sustainable growth, a mentor could have steered us toward more practical solutions. They could have helped us identify what was working and what wasn't, ensuring that we didn't burn through our funds prematurely.

Moreover, a mentor can provide emotional support during tough times. Entrepreneurship is an emotional rollercoaster, and having someone to lean on during the highs and lows can make a significant difference. They not only offer guidance on business decisions but also help you stay grounded, focused, and motivated when things get challenging.

Conclusion

As we move forward in the world of startups, it is crucial to recognize the importance of mentorship. While it's true that some entrepreneurs are able to succeed without a mentor, the vast majority of us benefit immensely from the wisdom and guidance of someone who has walked the path before us. Mentors help us avoid common pitfalls, save valuable time, and provide a fresh perspective on challenges we may not have anticipated.

In the world of entrepreneurship, a mentor is more than just a sounding board—they are a strategic partner who can make a world of difference. If you are serious about your startup's success, I strongly urge you to find a mentor, advisor, or guru who can guide you through the complexities of the entrepreneurial journey. Their lessons, based on their own experiences, will help you navigate your own path with greater confidence and clarity.

CHAPTER TWELVE

Family

Family—a small word that holds within it an entire universe. It encapsulates the joys, sorrows, challenges, and triumphs that shape our lives. My journey in entrepreneurship has taught me many lessons, but perhaps the most profound one is the importance of keeping your family close, involving them in your work, and sharing your dreams with them. It's a realization that came to me a bit late in my journey, but one that has transformed my perspective entirely.

I left home at the age of 16 to prepare for competitive exams. What followed were years of college life and then a job in Bangalore. The first 16 years of my life were the ones I spent most closely with my family. After that, my interactions with them became limited to occasional visits and phone calls. Life became a series of milestones—education, career, marriage, and eventually starting my own family. Yet, during these pivotal moments, I failed to see how integral family could be to my entrepreneurial journey.

As I ventured into the world of startups, I initially saw my business as something separate from my personal life. I thought of it as a domain where logic, strategy, and hard work would determine success, leaving little room for emotional connections. It was only much later, after facing setbacks, that I realized how wrong I was. Sharing your entrepreneurial journey with your family, discussing your ideas, and involving them in your decisions can lead to insights and emotional support that no external advisor can provide.

The person who taught me this invaluable lesson was my wife. Coming from a Sindhi business family, she carried a deeply ingrained belief in the power of family involvement. Her father, a successful businessman, followed traditions that symbolized this philosophy. One such ritual involved using a small silver spade during the ground-breaking ceremony of any new property purchase. Every family member would participate, symbolizing their collective blessings and involvement.

When I first saw this, I was intrigued and asked her about its significance. She explained, *"Once the family steps foot on the land and gives their blessings, success follows. It's about the energy and positivity they bring."* Her father also made it a point to consult her mother about every major business decision, regardless of her technical knowledge in the domain. The idea was not about expertise; it was about involvement, trust, and shared vision.

I used to quote stories of Steve Jobs, Warren Buffett, and other iconic figures to my wife, holding them as my role models. She would listen patiently, then gently remind me, "Role models should start at home—your parents, spouse, or siblings. For me and my brother, our father has always been our role model in business." At first, I didn't fully grasp the depth of her words, but over time, her perspective resonated deeply. She was right: the family's belief in you is unwavering, and their support is irreplaceable.

In our case, my Dad was the first person to trust us and offered us the initial and most crucial funding. There were zero questions asked while the cheque was handed and all we saw was belief and faith with which those hands guided us. I neglected to involve my family in critical aspects of the business. My dad, a seasoned professional with decades of experience in accountancy, compliance, and financial management, was someone I rarely consulted for advice. Looking back, this was a supremely missed opportunity. His wisdom could have helped me avoid some of the financial pitfalls, I encountered.

When we were wrapping up our business, I sat down with my wife and asked her candidly, "What do you think we did wrong?" Her response was eye-opening. She highlighted areas where we had overspent, strategies that lacked focus, and decisions that could have been approached differently. Had I engaged her and my family earlier in these conversations, I might have avoided some of the mistakes that ultimately led to our closure.

The energy that family provides is unparalleled. They are the ones who will stand by you when you're at your lowest and celebrate with you when you succeed. This emotional support is a reservoir of strength that every entrepreneur needs. Sharing your journey with your family doesn't mean burdening them with every detail but involving them enough to make them feel part of your mission.

My Advice to Fellow Entrepreneurs

To all the entrepreneurs out there, my advice is simple yet profound: keep your family close. Talk to them about your work, share your ideas, and involve them in your journey. They don't need to be experts in your field; their emotional support, perspectives, and blessings are often more valuable than technical advice.

Remember, the very reason you're working hard—whether to provide a better life for your children, support your parents, or fulfill a dream you share with your spouse—is rooted in family. Don't lose sight of this connection. Family is not just your safety net; they are your silent partners in success.

In entrepreneurship, we often talk about networking, mentorship, and funding, but we rarely emphasize the role of family. For me, this realization came late, but it's a lesson I'll carry forward in everything I do. As I look back on my journey, I see clearly that the strength, guidance, and love of my family have been my greatest assets. They are the reason I dream, the reason I persevere, and the reason I will try again. To every entrepreneur reading this: never underestimate the power of family. Share your journey with them—they are your biggest cheerleaders, your most honest critics, and the ones who will stand by you, no matter what.

If You Are New To Startups – A Comprehensive Guide

The entrepreneurial journey is as exciting as it is challenging. Here are some principles and tips to help you navigate this path with clarity and purpose. Whether you are contemplating your first startup or already on the journey, these insights will serve as a roadmap.

1. Follow Your Entrepreneurial Fire

If you have that nagging feeling, that constant itch to create something, listen to it. This isn't something you can explain to others, nor do you need to. It's personal. The desire to start something new stems from an inner passion that won't easily fade. Recognize it, embrace it, and act on it.

Remember, ideas alone are not enough—execution matters. Take small steps. Write down your ideas, research them, and brainstorm strategies to bring them to life. Even if your first idea doesn't succeed, the process will prepare you for the next.

2. Be Debt-Free

Debt can be a significant burden for any entrepreneur. When you're under financial strain, it becomes challenging to focus on innovation and growth. If you're serious about starting a business, ensure you're debt-free first.

Additionally:

Have at least 12 months of living expenses saved up, so you don't have to worry about survival while building your dream.

Get health insurance and emergency funds. In India especially, unplanned medical bills can derail your progress faster than you anticipate.

3. The Job vs. Startup Dilemma

Balancing a job with a startup is tricky. On the one hand, your job provides financial security; on the other, it limits the time and energy you can dedicate to your startup. Ask yourself:

Can I balance both for the next 12-18 months?

Do I have enough savings to quit my job and focus entirely on my startup?

If you choose to keep your job, structure your schedule carefully to dedicate consistent time to your startup. If you decide to quit, do so only after detailed financial planning. Having a safety net is not a luxury—it's a necessity.

4. Stay on Top of Government Compliance

Registering a business comes with a host of responsibilities, especially in India. From GST filings to maintaining proper financial records, you'll be juggling multiple compliance requirements. Ignoring these can result in hefty penalties and stress down the line.

Use tools or hire a consultant to ensure timely filings.

Keep your business organized from day one with proper bookkeeping.

Being proactive with legal obligations saves time and resources and ensures smooth scaling later.

5. Choose Your Co-Founder Wisely

Your co-founder is your partner in this journey. Misaligned visions or values can derail even the best ideas. Treat this decision as seriously as marriage:

Look for complementary skills. If you're strong in tech, find someone good at sales or marketing.

Assess compatibility. Do your working styles match?

Define roles clearly to avoid conflicts.

If you're someone who prefers complete control, consider going solo. It might mean slower growth, but it ensures fewer disputes and complete autonomy.

6. Embrace Minimalism

Start with a lean approach. Focus on what's essential and avoid unnecessary expenses. For instance:

Work from home instead of renting office space.

Use free or low-cost tools for operations until you have consistent revenue.

Delay hiring until absolutely necessary; instead, outsource to freelancers for specific tasks.

Every penny saved can be reinvested into the business for growth.

7. Be Confident About Your Product

Confidence is contagious. Whether pitching to a client, investor, or friend, talk about your product with conviction. If you're not sold on your product, why should anyone else be?

Develop a compelling narrative around your product.

Showcase how it solves a real problem.

Collect and highlight testimonials or success stories from early adopters.

Confidence builds trust, and trust leads to opportunities.

8. Don't Be a Jack of All Trades

It's tempting to do everything yourself, especially when funds are limited, but this approach often backfires. Acknowledge your limitations and delegate tasks to experts whenever possible.

Hire professionals for tasks like accounting, legal compliance, or web development if needed.

Focus your energy on areas where your expertise adds the most value.

Remember, your time is limited. Use it wisely.

9. Be Humble and Empathetic

Humility is a key trait of successful entrepreneurs. Arrogance alienates people, while humility builds lasting relationships. Treat your team, clients, and peers with respect. Celebrate their successes and learn from them.

Acknowledge contributions from your team and partners.

Stay grounded regardless of success or failure.

A positive and empathetic attitude creates goodwill that can open doors in unexpected ways.

10. Take Care of Your Mental and Physical Health

Running a startup can be all-consuming, but neglecting your well-being will harm both you and your business.

Practice mindfulness or meditation to manage stress.

Maintain a healthy work-life balance.

Exercise regularly and eat nutritious meals to stay energized.

A healthy founder is a productive founder.

11. Build Resilience

Failure is part of the process. Use setbacks as learning opportunities rather than reasons to quit. Every successful entrepreneur has faced failures—they're stepping stones to success.

Analyze what went wrong and take corrective action.

Stay focused on your long-term vision despite short-term challenges.

Persistence often separates successful entrepreneurs from the rest.

Final Words

Entrepreneurship is not just about the destination—it's about the journey. The lessons you learn, the people you meet, and the impact you create are invaluable. Remember:

Failure isn't fatal. It's a stepping stone.

Adapt, learn, and grow at every stage.

Believe in your vision, but always stay grounded.

You've got this. Trust the process, stay resilient, and enjoy the ride!

"You win some; you learn some. This time, I've learned, and hoping to move forward with each bit of that learning."

About The Author

Arpit Goel is a seasoned IT professional, with a strong focus on the Business Intelligence and Analytics domain. With a career rooted in technologies, Arpit has honed expertise in unraveling insights from complex systems and transforming them into impactful solutions.

Beyond a thriving career, Arpit has embarked on multiple entrepreneurial ventures, delving into the world of startups. While some ventures achieved modest success, others provided invaluable lessons that shaped Arpit's perspective on business, resilience, and growth. This journey of highs and lows has fueled his desire to share knowledge with aspiring entrepreneurs, empowering them to navigate the often challenging yet rewarding path of building businesses from the ground up.

You can connect with Arpit :

LinkedIn: www.linkedin.com/in/arpgoel

Instagram: techiebawarchi

Email: arpitgoel.2211@gmail.com

Whether you're a budding entrepreneur, a curious reader, or someone looking for insights into the startup ecosystem, Arpit is always eager to share stories and ideas.

www.ingramcontent.com/pod-product-compliance
Lightning Source LLC
LaVergne TN
LVHW041116150826
845673LV00007B/2072

* 9 7 9 8 8 9 6 3 2 6 8 5 4 *